IMPROV

ENJOY LIFE AND SUCCESS
WITH THE POWER OF YES

JOHN CREMER

SUNMAKERS

Text ©2009 John Cremer.

Design, layout and illustrations by Ayd Instone.

Published by Sunmakers, a division of Eldamar Ltd.

157 Oxford Road, Cowley, Oxford, OX4 2ES, UK

Tel +44(0)1865 779944

www.sunmakers.co.uk

Version 2.1

ISBN: 978-0-9553917-3-6

www.johncremer.co.uk

acknowledgements

Eternal gratitude to all the Maydays, past present and future for the laughter and learning:

Sab, Rachel, Guy, George, Rebecca, Professsor Zany, Prageet, Sarita, Katy, Tony, Jen, Robin, Mark, Jackie, Charlie, Alistair, Pete, Andy, David, Jason D, Heather, Jason B, Alexis, Laura, Piano Joe...

...and whoever shows up next.

To James Westly
Friend, mentor and teacher of Presence

CONTENTS

INTRODUCTION

This book is written as the result of saying "Yes" to requests from many of the hundreds of CEOs and business leaders with whom I have been fortunate enough to work.

Having been thrilled and inspired by the experience of improvising in front of an audience, usually for the first time, they want to take the magic back to the workplace. This is not simply for frivolous or entertaining reasons; business leaders have a sharp eye on the bottom line and recognise the value of an environment which promotes and supports workplace creativity. They see the truth in the words of leading authority on humour in the workplace, Kate Hull-Rodgers, who says, "People who have more fun get more done". I could not have put this better myself – so I won't try!

The purpose of this humble tome is to demystify the process of enticing a group of people to take risks and express their spontaneous creativity.

The chosen method is improvisation with a comedic element. Being "on the spot" without script or preparation compels us to be ourselves, and laughter is almost invariably the result, as nothing is funnier than human nature just as it is.

To create and maintain an arena conducive to productive improvisation requires an awareness and sensitivity in the presenter, as well as a toolkit of exercises. It is vital to understand the purpose of the various techniques in order to deliver them to maximum benefit, and also to be able to make use of the likely outcomes.

Fortunately, once we open the door to the human spirit we find an endless reserve of resilience and flexibility waiting to engage and explore.

Many major companies as well as SMEs are using improvisation techniques to transform the way they do business. Some of the many business benefits of this discipline are explored throughout the book. There are many layers to this work and the benefits tend to spill over in unexpected directions, even to the extent of triggering philosophical self examination in an organisation.

Why do we do it that way?

What are we really about?

Why not try this?

Does work have to be so boring?

What if we take a few more risks?

Once these new neural pathways open up, both the individual and the organisation become refreshed and energised, new possibilities emerge and the range of options widens.

Human beings have always flourished on the edge. In fact, as a species, we started to walk upright on the border between woodland and savannah. By using tools and developing agriculture we created stability and control of our environment. In modern Western life we can, finances permitting, live in a bubble where temperature, light levels, food supplies, entertainment, information availability and so on can all be controlled at the flick of a switch. However, most of us are not that happy. We are built to be challenged, puzzled, thrilled and surprised, yet find ourselves in a world where art, movies, music, stories, food, clothing etc. are all mass produced, processed and easily available.

Our experiences are second hand at best, as even Hollywood films are often the results of testing by focus groups. We control our world but, it is, increasingly, two dimensional and sanitised. Cocooned in this security, we are torn between staying safe and seeking new frontiers. If we always settle for what we know then boredom and apathy result.

Companies innovate to carve out a solid presence in the marketplace, then put procedures in place to maintain their position. If they are successful in this then their employees become dispirited and fearful. By applying the paradoxical improvisational discipline of "safe risk" organisations can revive their creative spirit and adapt to ever changing market conditions.

By having a go at improvising and being willing to make mistakes you will discover dormant talents for storytelling, entertaining, creating, letting go, empathising, amusing, bouncing back, feeling and laughing,
 i.e. being more alive.

You have been improvising since birth and will continue to do so for the remainder of your life. May it be a full and happy one.

John's work with the Executive Team at T-Mobile was particularly energising and enjoyable. It enabled profound learning about leadership styles, interaction and communication. This was done in a safe and supportive environment and had a lasting impact on both the whole team and the individuals in it.

— Asher Rickayzen
Director of Enterprise Planning & Delivery, T-Mobile UK

OVERVIEW

The book is divided into three 'Acts'.

Act One

This covers some of my personal life-journey in connection with improvisation. It is a path shared by many improvisers, which starts in the spontaneous flow of childhood, goes through increasing restriction and adaptation to social norms and expectations and then opens out into flow again, with the added understanding and experience of the journey so far. This is an infinitely refreshing process where one never arrives or "gets it" but simply seeks more willingness to learn.

There are also some reflections on common threads I have picked up on the path; themes that have informed my travels and given me tools and insights to assist my fellow travellers. Some of these themes are philosophical or psychological and will hopefully shed some light on the influences which restrict our spontaneous creativity.

It is tempting to judge these obstacles and wish they had never been there, yet in many ways they are the grains of sand in the oyster shell which become pearls. Somehow our creative magical spirit is able to survive chronic deprivation for years or decades and then spring onto the stage at the right moment and dazzle not just the audience but our own limited picture of ourselves.

This is the alchemical process which part two is designed to trigger.

Act Two

I give some of the exercises that I have used with groups over the past fifteen years. These exercises are simple enough that if you have picked up this book by mistake, having no interest in or exposure to improvisation (maybe you misread the title as "Improve" and think it's a self-help book) you can use them right now. Whether at a sales meeting, a birthday party, down the pub or anywhere there are a few people gathered, with a few moments and an ounce of willingness – you can do this.

Every exercise is walked through step by step and there is also some context given:

- what you can expect to see
- how to build on what emerges if you wish
- how to support people
- the possible business applications.

You can jump straight to part two and make it happen if you wish. Then, if you are intrigued by what emerges, part one will give some insights into the processes at work.

Act Three

This is a list of resources for further reading and exploration which I have encountered over the years. It's not exhaustive, just books, troupes, theatres, teachers and organisations that I happen to like and value. I only recommend resources that I have personally used or teachers that I have trained with. The list grows exponentially as more people and organisations come to value this wonderful discipline.

I have included my email address, so if you have enjoyed this book, let me know. If you didn't enjoy it, then you may well have a better one inside you. Please write it soon and send me a copy. Lastly - if I can help you on your journey, please ask.

Act One

MY JOURNEY

As a young lad in middle class Brighton, I remember it was considered highly important to know what you wanted to be when you grew up. This always puzzled me, and I felt something lacking within myself when around those who knew they wanted to be a vet or train driver. Human behaviour was largely a mystery to me and, having a philosophical nature, I pondered the purpose of life from an early age. At around seven years old I came to the conclusion that the purpose of life was to go on holiday as that was the time my parents looked forward to the most, and when they were most carefree, energised and excited. This helped me a bit but did not readily explain the other 50 weeks in the year. Much of the adult activity around me seemed guided by perverse circular reasoning, whereby people lived in order to go to work to earn money in order to live and so on. Outside of that perpetual loop, you went on holiday, but not often and not for long. It all seemed absurd and pointless.

Revelation came shortly afterwards when I watched Monty Python's Flying Circus for the first time. Suddenly the absurdity I had observed was not just in my head; there it all was being ridiculed, on screen and by grownups! I felt simultaneously understood, validated and hugely entertained. It was as if the whole power structure had been inverted and the naughtiest boys in school had been given the attention of the whole country instead of being stifled and punished.

Thursday night became the highlight of my existence. I would watch *Top of the Pops, Tomorrows World, Colditz* and then the pinnacle – *Monty Python*. On Fridays the playground would be awash with the more enlightened boys doing silly walks to the amusement of the cognoscenti and the bewilderment of those not in the know. My life path was now clear, I would do my O-levels, then A-levels, leave school at a respectable eighteen years old then simply apply and join the Monty Python team as their youngest member.

In 1973 I sat in reverential awe in the Brighton Dome watching live onstage *Monty Python's First Farewell Tour*. Sadly, cracks had begun to appear in my life path when John Cleese left after the third series and then, after the fourth series, they disbanded. I was genuinely bereft; no matter how unrealistic my plan, it was all I had. *Fawlty Towers* was small compensation to one so crushed by the whims of fate. Looking back I can see only one glimmer throughout my education. At 12 years old, in "Ernie" Pascoe's English class, we were split into teams and asked to write and perform our own performance. Of course we came up with a Pythonesque half hour of skits. Though I say so myself, it was a fine show for a group of 12 year olds and I still remember who was in it and some magical moments when we were truly alive. This was the last gasp of creative ether before my head and body sank beneath the tide of 1970's British mediocrity. I next came up for air in 1985 after I had moved to Arizona for a change of scenery from Thatcher's Britain. My father had moved there and gave me a place to stay. He also told me that a friend of his had experienced a powerful weekend workshop which anyone could attend at no cost.

This was called Omega Vector and was run by a remarkable man called George Addair. George was a Southern Baptist minister who decided there was more to his life than condemning people to Hell, so went on a quest. He attended every human potential training that was available and distilled his own version which he offered as a service to humanity. The training has been running for over 30 years, has never charged a penny and has positively impacted the lives of many thousands of people.

For me it was a revelation, brand new yet totally familiar and the messages I came away with were simple yet also profound – I saw that the quality of our lives is a direct result of how we treat other people, that everything in our lives comes from others and that we isolate ourselves and manipulate others at great personal cost. I realised I had withdrawn from people, played it safe and only reached out when I wanted something from someone, I was a "taker" and during the workshop saw clearly that "givers" win and "takers" lose. At the start of the training we each had to stand in turn and say why we were there. I shook with fear during this process. At a later part of the training we were split into pairs and encouraged to take a risk by performing for two minutes for the rest of the group. When it came to my turn to perform, the fear was still there but I committed to give it my all. I still recall every second of that two minute performance and many of the other ones also; we were more alive then.

Let us fast forward to 1993. I found myself in the Star Theatre, Scottsdale, Arizona attending a performance of the *Oxymorons Improvised Comedy Troupe*. Fifty people were packed into a smallish room behind a New Age bookshop, where the air conditioning unit was ill suited to the task of cooling the room, so we stuck to the plastic lawn chairs.

The lights dimmed and a bald rotund Italian-American man came to the front of the room, established instant rapport with the audience and created a warm expectation. This was the legendary director Louis Anthony Russo.

A troupe of eight people bounded onto to the stage and the show began. Taking audience suggestions they effortlessly created scenes and skits in the style of "Whose Line is it Anyway?" Characters, situations and hilarity flowed from one to the other, there were no pauses or back tracking and the show ended with two actors becoming a two-headed being recounting an adventure by speaking alternating words in the story. I was spellbound.

Louis returned to the stage and announced "If you want to do this yourself we teach classes every Wednesday." I signed up on the spot and Wednesday became my new Thursday but, instead of watching the entertainment, I was in it and learning fast.

One evening we were working on limericks which, typically, are written by one person sitting and thinking. In the world of improvisation, five people stand in a line, the audience shouts out a subject and the troupe create the limerick, one line each on the spot. It must rhyme, scan, make sense and, ideally, be funny. I was the first person in line and the suggestion was "bikers". I dutifully stepped forward with the first line "Bikers, they like to have fun". The combination of my cheerful demeanour, English accent and the image of bikers made the rest of the class fall about laughing. Louis told me to start again, with the same result. I had no idea why they found it so funny but every time I delivered the line, the funnier it became until we finally limped, gasping, through the limerick. This gave me a taste for working an audience for laughter.

The beauty of improvisation lies in the simplicity, there are a few basic rules underpinning the process and, when you follow the rules, it works. The rules open up a zone of flow and connectivity where the scene is discovered from within, rather than assembled from ideas and actions. It is both exhilarating and nurturing to spend time in this zone. One Wednesday I was invited to join the advanced class which was held on Mondays. My week now had two peaks. I was actually in a class with the people I had admired performing and, one glorious Monday, I was invited to be in a show.

A big part of improvisation training is to say "Yes". This is not a natural part of British culture where we are rigorously trained to respond with an immediate "No" to any suggestion put of our comfort zone. If pressed, we then invent reasons not to do something. On this occasion I said "Yes" and have been saying "Yes" ever since.

My first show; same steamy room, same plastic chairs - only this time I was at the back of the room waiting to go on stage. The show was going really well, and we were flying. Halfway through, we were acting a scene called "Epic Novel". The structure was, that Louis was writing a novel, speaking his thoughts out loud and the troupe were performing his ideas. In this case, it was a tale of disaster, set on an aeroplane. The scene was wobbling so Louis announced dramatically, "Only one passenger could save the plane! A British passenger stepped forward with his solution". The troupe shrank away from me as I stepped forward and delivered a truly appalling solution - but with the same panache I had brought to the biker limerick in class. The audience loved it, while I relished the laughter and learned a lot about stepping out empty handed, with nothing but commitment. The shows were every Friday and

Saturday night and I was in all of them. My week now had more peaks than troughs.

After a couple of hundred shows, I was invited to audition for a troupe who performed Playback Theatre - a form of improvised theatre, based on stories from the audience, which has its roots in Psychodrama. We were not playing for laughs as the stories were often gritty, and the only restriction was that they were the true and actual experience of the storyteller.

Our range of audiences was truly diverse. One day I remember, we performed at a shelter for teenage runaways in a tough part of town in the morning, and then in the evening, we were at the best hotel around, performing for a large corporation. We performed constantly, sometimes three shows a day, continually honing our skills and building trust in each other.

The troupe itself was diverse. Our director was a Jewish topless dancer and the actors a Samoan lesbian, a flamboyantly gay Mexican man, who knew every Broadway show tune ever written, a gay black Voodoo priest who could retell an entire story with just movement, a Native American woman and myself – the token, straight, white boy. Our musician was a recovering crack addict, fresh from prison, whom we met while doing a show at a homeless shelter. We were rarely bored.

In 2001, after a personal meltdown, I returned home to England. My business and health had collapsed and I stepped off the plane with no job, money, bank account, car, house or plan. I was 39 years old. From a socio-economic perspective things were not good. From an improvisational perspective, things were just perfect – I was once again stepping empty handed into the void and anything could happen. I gave myself two disciplines. Firstly, I would not do anything I did not love, and secondly, I would not run for a bus. If the bus left before I walked to it, I would get the next one or walk. I refused to hurry. Looking back I see that I had given myself space and time for something new to emerge.

So often we fill every waking moment with being busy and leave no room for the mysterious to unfold in our lives. The part of us that has been trained to justify our existence, through activity, takes over the show and the deeper self gets ignored.

With love and support from my family I was able to "come home" on many levels and start a richer, more authentic phase of my life. Again I was drawn to the edge.

I enrolled on a five month course in Permaculture, which is a way of building sustainable communities, and quickly became the class clown and MC of the social events. One of the principles of Permaculture is that in any ecosystem, it is always at the edge that it is the most productive. So, for example, a tidal area will sustain more species per square yard than the adjacent land or sea. Living in Arizona I had seen one of Earth's richest habitats – an ancient Riparian woodland set between desert and river bank.

The course lead me to a stint as a volunteer, helping to build a straw bale and chestnut wood house in coppice woodland. The owner, Ben Law, had followed his dream of building a truly sustainable house on his own land, mostly from the raw materials growing on site. He faced tremendous obstacles during a ten year fight for planning permission, which is outlined is his superb book *The Woodland House*. For a project so "off the grid" to succeed, Ben had necessarily gathered a huge number of volunteers and supporters to his remote woodland. His story was featured on Channel 4s show, *Grand Designs*, and was the most popular episode ever shown.

Standing there watching the filming, on the edge, between traditional woodcraft and high tech national media, the learning was reinforced – that everything comes to us through other people. There is a beautiful phrase in the King James - "Where there is no vision the people perish".

I have come to believe that the reverse is also true. We all have dreams and visions that we wish to achieve, but if we cannot inspire and connect with other people, then the vision does not come to fruition. We could also say, "Where there are no people the vision perishes". I continued to make efforts to connect with more people, including attending an active meditation, one Sunday, which was based on the teachings of Osho, an Indian mystic dedicated to encouraging people to live and express more fully.

At the end of the session the hosts announced that they were part of a community in Dorset, called Osho Leela and were building an eco-house. They asked if anyone wanted to come down and help, and my response was the inevitable "Yes".

Working on the house was an opportunity to observe this vibrant community, and I soon signed up to take part in a year long intensive training designed to deepen connections to oneself and other people. This training comprised one long weekend per month plus a thirty day residential intensive in Holland at the end.

Each weekend was a total blast, no holds barred, nonstop, energetic, challenging, exhausting and liberating. Part of every weekend was a series of theatrical performances, usually beginning at 3am, by groups of participants. We were encouraged to value enthusiasm over technique and, with most of those attending having no acting training, the results were not theatrically sound, but were enormous fun to watch and to play in.

Six months into the course I was approached by a fellow participant. He informed me that after a long process of elimination he had worked out that the best skit in each weekend had a common factor – me. He had noticed that when I was in a skit, it had structure, timing, laughs and a storyline and said that if I ever decided to teach these skills he would be the first to sign up. A seed was planted, an itch I could not scratch.

I decided to teach improvised comedy as I had learned it from Louis, so I rented a grotty room above a pub and charged £4 per head for a 2 hour class every Thursday. If 6 people came I felt rich. Imagine earning £24 for doing something you love. The class grew and grew, people became regulars and, once there was a hard core, we decided to do a show in the Brighton Festival in June 2004.

We rented a 50 seater theatre, called ourselves the Mayday Players and the show sold out – at £5 a head! This was really living large. We did another show and sold out again, so we made it a monthly event. After the fourth show all our friends had been to see us, so we had to work hard at promoting it.

Meanwhile, in 2003, Osho Leela had approached me to teach taster classes at their Summer Festival. These were such a huge success, we decided to run a weekend workshop, which sold out in two days, so we added another. Things were cooking.

In July 2004 I went to Holland for the 30 day intensive which would complete my one year training. It had been noticed that I still had the habit of hanging back in social situations and I resolved to break this pattern. The residential intensive is called the "Wow" and is designed to break down internal barriers to experiencing life more immediately; my commitment was to say "Yes" for 30 days continually. There were 90 of us from around the world, we slept in dorms and everything was communal. We experienced sleep deprivation (an average of 3 hours sleep per night for 30 days including 4 all night sessions), dance marathons, catharsis, interpersonal friction, occasional visits to the outside world, love affairs, meditations and, of course, utterly bizarre theatre performances. Something shifted within me and the challenge was to maintain the shift after leaving.

I headed straight to Osho Leela and taught improv at the Summer Festival.

During one class a fellow called Prasadam put his head round the door, observed proceedings, nodded and left. I decided to attend one of his Zen Theatre classes, which take place completely in the moment, with no plan or structure, and can go in any direction from tragic to hilarious and back again in moments. We hit it off like long lost soul mates and he approached me and asked if I would like to do a show with him. Inevitably I said "Yes".

He arranged a performance space for that evening and we agreed to meet for dinner to talk about the show. At dinner I asked him what we would do in the show. He looked at me, a devilish twinkle in his eye and said "I don't know". He meant it.

At 9pm we walked on stage in front of 100 people and started the show, having never worked together before and having just met that afternoon. All we had was commitment and the rules of improvisation; it went down a storm. Afterwards he told me he was about to start a thirty day residential Zen Theatre training and would I like to attend. Of course it was another "Yes".

This turned out to be a whole new level of improvising - thirty days unfolding, moment to moment, following whatever emerged, be it absurd notions or deeply buried emotional trauma, with the only restriction being that no violence was permitted. By removing the typical boundaries of social norms, living away from the outside world and expressing what comes, it is inevitable that transformation occurs. I left with a clear sense that my destiny was to teach improvisation wherever there is the demand. I also had a phone number to call.

During the festival a woman approached me to ask if I would work in the business world. She was part of a peer learning group for business owners and felt the skills would be highly useful to decision makers. After the usual "Yes", I found myself well out of my comfort zone running a half day session in a very prestigious bank in the City of London for 25 chief executives. I was terrified; they loved it. This one event lead to more engagements and my thriving career as a trainer and speaker for businesses. I have now worked with hundreds of CEOs and major companies. The demand for this work is growing rapidly, as the same skills required to improvise onstage are absolutely vital for running a business, working with teams, engaging with clients, problem solving and generally being more present and alive.

When I first started in the business world, I was seen as a total maverick and many potential clients would back away when I told them what I did. I recently spoke to a group of CEOs, and the chairman of the group confided in me that he had seen my initial showcase to the company in 2004. Back then, in answer to the question "Would you book this speaker to talk to your group?", he had written "No never", in large capital letters! Times have changed and I am regularly approached by highly mainstream organisations and government departments.

In 2007 I was awarded Star Speaker by the Academy for Chief Executives and in 2008, I was made a Fellow of the Professional Speakers Association.

The Mayday Players have gone from strength to strength and are now called the Maydays. We perform regularly for public and corporate audiences, and offer training in all elements of improvisation, having been trained ourselves by some of the very best. We won Best Comedy Show 2007 Brighton Fringe Festival. As a troupe we have generated a thriving improvisation community in Brighton, having trained and helped establish several other troupes here and in London. We may well be the only improv troupe to have received a testimonial from the Bishop of Norwich, after performing for 200 Norfolk vicars at an ecclesiastical conference. Once a month we still do a show in a grotty room above a pub.

the task in hand

In our modern Western culture we have inherited a way of living life that appears odd to other cultures. Our material needs are largely met without too much struggle or effort, as many of us can earn a reasonable living without even breaking a sweat on the job. Heavy labour is performed by machinery so we no longer till the soil by hand and we generally do not harvest or slaughter our own food. Physically we are remote from the basic struggle of survival; we can order food online and have it delivered; fresh clean water is piped into our home and light and warmth appear at the flick of a switch. We don't have to get our hands dirty. Emotionally we are growing increasingly distant from each other. It is quite easy to spend long stretches of time without speaking to a living human being and still meet all our material needs.

Young people spend hours interacting with screens, on their mobile phones and computers; they seem more quickly, yet less deeply, connected. Those of working age are busier than ever, responding to multiple demands for their attention and are expected to be available 24/7. For many working people it is hard for them to see their work as having a positive impact on the world; it is just something they do to pay the bills in order to survive.

Older people are simply marginalised, often bewildered by the pace of technological change. Their wisdom and experience is no longer seen as having a unique and valuable contribution to make to society.

Mentally we have been programmed to the see the world and ourselves in certain ways. The Sufis call this "The Cultural Trance".

Our education system focuses on filling up simplistic parts of our intelligence while ignoring or suppressing far more creative and inspired faculties.

The greatest obstacle to inspiration is duality. Our minds have a basic and necessary ability to recognise pairs of opposites e.g. day and night, left and right, male and female etc. This binary processing is a handy foundation for teaching young children how to comprehend differences. Sadly, much of our culture has never gone beyond this phase of development and cannot get beyond thinking in two, so much of our thinking is determined by right and wrong, good and bad and so on.

In learning there is, of course, one correct answer to the sum of 2 plus 2. There is only one capital city of France – Paris is the right answer; all other answers are wrong. Where we trip ourselves up is any area outside of the absolute. What's the right colour for a wall, for example?

In order to control a classroom of 30 children, stick to the curriculum and get pupils to pass the obligatory tests, teachers face a hugely difficult task. They must programme the children with the "right" answer so it can be regurgitated on demand.

There is a subtle yet insidious blending that occurs. "Right" gets associated with "good". When the child gets the right answer, the teacher responds "That's good". The child often hears this as "I'm good". Conversely "wrong" and "bad" get stuck together. Children rapidly learn to adapt and seek positive attention, because they are motivated by deep survival mechanisms to get the answers "right" and be seen as "good".

Every human being requires attention to survive on all levels. If the parents of a small child totally ignore it, then it will starve and die. Emotionally we all need positive attention in order to thrive and develop. Mentally we need the attention of a teacher or mentor in order to learn. With a programme in place that strongly reinforces that there is one right answer and that getting it wrong will bring negative attention, shame and illogically, but instinctively, possible death, it is no wonder that many children live in terror of not knowing the square root of sixteen when asked by the teacher. Most schools are not devoted to developing the unique creative potential of the individual child. They are instead churning out compliant, walking filing cabinets stuffed with dualistic information.

With Health and Safety rules relentlessly squelching any activity that holds any possibility of danger, the opportunities for children to have an immediate experience of the physical world are rapidly diminishing.

Lame Deer was a medicine man in the Sioux tribe, living on a reservation with about the worst levels of poverty and alcoholism in the USA. His definition of cultural deprivation was to be a white child growing up in middle class suburbia!

After a decade or more of this lop-sided education, it is time for us to head out into the world to earn a living, often without the social skills or emotional intelligence to interact with the people who could help us succeed. Terrified of doing or saying the wrong thing, we shrink ourselves and our experience of life down to that which is acceptable. It is no wonder workplaces are full of demotivated and dispirited people keeping their heads down and waiting for the weekend, or their holiday, or retirement so they can live a little. We English are especially adept at this behaviour.

I have often gone into a company to give some improvisation training to a team or department and found that someone really struggles with the process. With some gentle probing they can actually recall the specific incident and teacher that shut them down. Once they are willing to take a small risk or two, with the support of the group, then miracles occur and the creative magic comes spilling out, often to the astonishment of the group. By the end, they are often the person standing, with face glowing and eyes shining, while their colleagues congratulate them for stepping up. I am absolutely not condemning teachers, who do a superb job in the face of overwhelming odds because, in my view it is the whole system that needs dismantling and rebuilding on a totally different basis.

Albert Einstein had a few pertinent things to say on this topic:

"We can't solve problems by using the same kind of thinking we used when we created them."

"The only thing that interferes with my learning is my education."

"One had to cram all this stuff into one's mind for the examinations, whether one liked it or not. This coercion had such a deterring effect on me that, after I had passed the final examination, I found the consideration of any scientific problems distasteful to me for an entire year."

"Imagination is more important than knowledge."

"Education is what remains after one has forgotten everything he learned in school."

CREATIVITY

One of the noticeable after effects of our education system is a phrase I hear countless times when talking to participants before a session or on tea break. They will chat with me and then lead into something which sounds a lot like this:

"This improv stuff is all well and good, and I enjoyed *Whose Line is it Anyway?* on television, but you have to be quick and clever to do that stuff and, well, I'm just not creative".

Our culture has so stifled and ignored the creative potential of most individuals that we now do it to ourselves. We do our jobs and earn a living and then pay good money to be *entertained* by *creative* types. We assume that they have something that we lack, pay them handsomely and give them license to act strangely because they are artists, those mythical creatures who breathe different air from us mortal beings.

As a 12 year old I remember sitting in "Killer" Reeves art class, staring at a blank sheet, after he'd given each of us paper, pencil and paints along with the instruction to "Paint something".

All around me boys scribbled and painted furiously while I sat bewildered, as I could not think of a single idea.

Finally, he discovered my lack of activity and I confessed my failure. He suggested I paint the water cycle i.e. rain falls, flows into rivers, river to sea, sea evaporates to make clouds and so on. I dutifully painted away and got by.

What if he had spent a moment, asked me what I was interested in and helped me discover my own theme? It would not have taken long and I would not have reinforced the judgement I held which was "I can't come up with ideas".

Through improvisation I have discovered an abundance of creativity in myself and every person I have ever worked with. The biggest challenge in working with the Maydays is killing creative projects because we generate so many and they are all great!

Experiment — *reach out and pick up the nearest object you can hold in one hand. Now come up with ten things you could do with that object other than its intended purpose, if the ideas are silly, dangerous, embarrassing or illegal then give yourself bonus points for your creativity. It's always there.*

Don't Pay Attention

Our greatest resource is our attention and it is the one we squander most thoughtlessly. Anyone who is truly successful in their field is consciously managing and directing their attention. In any human endeavour, it is the people who choose where they consistently focus their attention who triumph, whether it is in sports, the arts, research or any area of business.

The entire advertising industry is solely concerned with where human attention is landing and remaining for even milliseconds. Branding seeks to attract our attention and manage our perceptions of a product or company.

Commercial television does not sell products; I have never bought toothpaste from Channel 4. Channel 4 seeks to sell my attention to toothpaste manufacturers. Commercial television sells our attention to advertisers because it has actual financial value.

Google has, of course, taken this to another level. By tracking our online searches they are following the trail of our attention and recording what we looked at and for how long. They know exactly what holds our attention and sell this to specific clients.

Highly effective managers and presenters know how to hold and direct the attention of their team or audience, but to do this they must first be able to direct their own attention. Human attention is a form of energy which can be sensed.

Experiment — *stare at someone in public when they are reading a newspaper, before too long they will look around to see who is looking at them. This is a good time to look away by the way! We sense human attention upon us.*

In the world of human interaction we find that attention precedes action. If there is a humanitarian crisis in another country and it appears as the top item on the national news, then resources will be sent to that country. Planes will be taking off with food and medicines and people will be collecting money to help out. If the same crisis happens on the same day that another bigger drama occurs in the news, then the response will not be so immediate or effective.

The level of response is proportional to the level of attention that is evoked. Attention is the key to all human resources and action follows attention. As we are bombarded by images seeking to grab our attention, we put more effort into screening them out, so we have less attention focussed in the present moment.

Thus advertising becomes more strident and intrusive, so we screen it out more, and so on. When we acquire the habit of not bringing attention to the present moment we do not live fully. Our senses are dull and we miss the subtle beauty of life on Earth. We are encouraged to live in an imagined better future, but this creates an insidious trap called "I'll be happy when...."

"I'll be happy when....I earn more money."

"I'll be happy when....I have a less stressful job."

"I'll be happy when....I retire."

"I'll be happy when....I get married."

"I'll be happy when....I get divorced."

"I'll be happy when...I have kids."

"I'll be happy when....the kids leave home."

We experience this process on a small scale when, for example, we are looking forward to going on holiday. Our attention is on the destination and the first cocktail by the pool. We can almost taste it, feel the sun on our skin, and anticipate that we won't have to think about work or the house for two weeks. So, our attention is not at work or at home in the lead up to the holiday. We want to be there and not here. It's when we arrive at the promised destination, and are about to sip that first cocktail, we remember the vital email we did not send, or we are not sure we turned off the oven, because we weren't present. Suddenly, we are physically on holiday, but our attention is at work or in the house and, no matter how much we may want to drag every scrap of attention to the poolside, it will keep going back to that email, then the oven. Coming home after two weeks, to a fused oven and unpleasant fallout from that unsent vital email, we start wishing we were still on holiday, by the pool......

Attention is like a muscle that we can exercise and use to bring ourselves repeatedly into the present moment. Unfortunately most of us have never been trained to do this. In fact, when we were young and full of energy and enthusiasm, we were sitting behind a desk in school daydreaming......

One of the benefits of improvisation is that it both requires and rewards presence. To improvise effectively our attention must be in the here and now. In fact, so much attention is required that, any wandering, planning or regret results in an instant onstage train wreck.

Successful improvisation creates more presence in both audience and performer, which intensifies the improvisation because a thrilling feedback loop is established, which can only be maintained by presence.

A lack of engagement in the workplace costs the economy billions every year, while a lack of engagement in one's own life carries an even higher price tag.

By being willing to take a few mild risks and even attempt to follow a few simple improvisation rules, we can reclaim our aliveness and tap into an endless spring of talent inside us. Once this taste is acquired, it is difficult to return to the mundane and be as satisfied by it as we once were.

Your attention is your greatest personal resource; it is the key to making clear choices in your life, to accessing your talents and connecting with other people. Once we become aware of the value of our attention, we can use it more effectively and not be hypnotised by any passing fancy gadget or drama. So guard it with your life, in many ways your attention is your life. So don't pay attention!

Life or Death

In working with groups of people new to improvisation, it is important to be able to manage the fear and anxiety which naturally arises. I make that sure I perform regularly with the Maydays and we take classes from teachers who stretch and challenge us. This maintains an empathy with the people we teach. I feel it is hypocritical to ask people to take risks that I do not frequently take myself. When a participant is nervous or even terrified, I know exactly how they are feeling so, I can engage with them and support them through the process. Let us examine the particular range of sensations, thoughts and emotions that a person has, sitting in an audience, knowing that it will soon be their turn to get up and have a go "onstage".

Physically: their heart rate increases, breathing quickens and is shallow, mouth becomes dry, hands shake, pupils dilate and face goes white as adrenaline is pumped into the bloodstream.

Emotionally: there is rising terror and a desire to escape. They will feel vulnerable and inadequate and ashamed to admit and acknowledge this.

Mentally: panic sets in, the mind is racing with disconnected thoughts. Very often negative messages from the past, memories of previous humiliations and vivid visualisation of an impending public disaster loom into focus.

Overall this is not a state conducive to productive improvisation with a positive outcome and must be addressed at all levels. Trite verbal reassurances such as "Go on, it won't be that bad" or "You'll be fine" actually make it worse.

Paul MacLean, former director of the Laboratory of the Brain and Behavior at the United States Institute of Mental Health suggests that the human brain is actually three brains in one, each of which was established successively in response to evolutionary need.

These three layers are the reptilian system, or R-complex, the limbic system, and the neocortex. Each layer is geared toward separate functions of the brain, but the layers interact substantially.

In our nervous first-time improviser we must speak to the reptilian brain, the basic survival mechanism of the human organism. It is a structure that has been around for about 300 million years and is highly effective at keeping a body alive. Especially relevant here is the "fight or flight" response when under perceived threat. This is the part producing physical effects.

We must also communicate with their limbic system or mammalian brain which is primarily concerned with strong emotion and relationship to others. This is the source of feeling out of the "clan" and rejected before they even speak. Meanwhile the neocortex; which is processing sensory information, planning and thinking away like mad, is busily producing all sorts of excuses and justifications and triggering negative emotional memories from the limbic system.

I always like to take a step back and look from a long term perspective - very long term.

Homo sapiens, in their current form, have been around and survived successfully for about 100,000 years. For 97% of that time we lived in small bands as hunter gatherers. When a lone human met a band of humans there was one prime question to ask at that point – "Are they going to kill and possibly eat me?" Every part of their attention was focussed on reading clues and assessing the likely response of the larger group.

You can experience this walking alone at night and encountering a group of strangers. All of a sudden you find yourself in a state of vigilance, where you monitor constantly and minutely, yourself and the group. All three brains are working together to ensure your survival. If the group gives you a friendly nod you carry on homewards and the reptilian brain sends calming chemicals into your bloodstream, so your limbic system can return to replaying an argument with your partner while your neocortex plans what to watch on TV.

To invite someone to improvise in front of a group may seem like no big deal but, to a large proportion of them, it is a life or death situation. From the perspective of the reptilian brain the group may turn on them and kill them, so it is no use saying, "Oh give it a go, what's the worst thing that could happen?" Logically they know they may feel a bit silly and not as good as their colleagues but, instinctively and emotionally, they sense and feel they will be permanently ostracised and killed. What to do?

As a facilitator, now that we have this understanding, we must begin every session by setting the scene, building trust and reassuring all three brains of all participants, before we invite people to improvise.

Here's a relevant learning experience from my journey. I was working with a company that had grown rapidly, from a small family business of 10 people to 35 employees and rising, in 18 months. The owner was determined to keep the family feeling and make all the employees feel part of the larger family rather than simply someone showing up for work. I came in just before Christmas, so we could present the session as a bit of fun, a celebration of a successful year and also a wee bit of training and bonding. They had kept the content as a nice surprise for the company, but informed me that everyone there liked a laugh and would be up for it. After meeting the group and setting the scene it was time to start improvising.

I always start with simple basic steps which involve everyone participating in the same process together and supporting each other. By the way, most improvisation exercises look ridiculous and pointless on paper and only come alive in practice; this is definitely one of them.

In this case, I had groups of five people come to the front of the room where each one in turn would deliver a short line and be applauded by the audience. I call this one *Stand and Deliver.* It was flowing, the audience was enjoying it and those who had delivered their line were glowing with a blend of relief and excitement. I invited the fifth batch of people to the front, and four jumped up but one woman, let us call her Sue, was frozen in her seat.

This particular exercise is crafted in such a way that for those who are nervous it is actually easier to just get up and do it than draw attention to oneself by refusing. 99.99% of the time I will engage with the person who is holding back, the group will want them to succeed and they will be able to take a breath and dive in.

In this case I observed that Sue was deep in fear. She had all the physical symptoms; white face, dilated pupils and shaking. This was a pivotal moment.

There is no-one to fall back on, the group was looking to me for leadership and this woman's well-being was in my hands. Sue had obviously had embarrassing public experiences and, at this moment, was telling herself that the whole group was thinking all the negative things that she was saying to herself. She was trapped in a virtual reality where the group was hostile and about to confirm how useless and untalented she really was. My agenda was to bring her on board and have a nice tidy session where everyone had taken part.

Fortunately, I was able to take a breath, drop my agenda and really listen to her; I asked the obvious question

"Sue, is this a bit much for you?"

Sue nodded – literally unable to speak.

Next question "Are you any good at clapping?"

A nod and a glimmer of a smile

"Can you laugh at the funny bits?"

Bigger nod, a wider smile and an audible release of breath.

"Well Sue, I have a vital role if you choose to play it. Can you laugh at the funny bits and clap at the right moments to keep us on track please?"

Sue whispered "Yes" and the entire group resumed breathing.

All three parts of Sue's brain were back onboard, because her panic response had been addressed without making it "wrong". Her emotional bond with the group had actually been enhanced. I believe human beings are innately driven to help each other and mentally she had a purpose and a way to contribute. To put a cherry on the top I extended an invitation to her - "If you get bored clapping and laughing and feel an overwhelming urge to come up front and join in, then please do." Sue's response was priceless "Yeah right!" She had now made a joke, with the whole group and the big scary facilitator, about the very situation that, a few moments ago, had been so uncomfortable.

One of the formulas I have heard used to describe humour is – Tragedy + Time = Comedy.

Once we had diffused the tension and averted a potential disaster, then the session flowed and had been enriched by Sue's process. The group as a whole felt safer and more bonded.

I am frequently brought in by companies who want team building without people climbing rock walls or shooting each other with paint balls. Which are popular ways of bonding teams through risk. I half jokingly promote my work in this realm by saying that the quickest and most effective way to bond a team is through a shared ordeal in the face of a common enemy; as an improvisation facilitator I provide both at once!

The Way Through

It only takes a few simple tools to scratch through the cultural trance and tap into the endless stream of creativity within us all. My shorthand for what emerges in improvisation is to refer to it as "the magic". Somehow, when we get into the flow, trust, take risks and follow a few basic guidelines, then something indefinable enters the room and takes us to unexpected places. By setting the scene, and being willing and open, we invite a more vivid atmosphere to engulf us.

I rely on three techniques to support productive improvisation. They allow absolute beginners to step out and taste the magic.

At the other extreme, when I perform with seasoned improvisers and it just doesn't fly then it is, inevitably, because one or more actors are not following one or more of these three techniques. We can invariably carry out an autopsy on a dud scene and see where it floundered.

The three techniques I use as basics, with an exploration of each, are detailed in the following three chapters.

LISTEN

A vital skill on many levels and with numerous applications, this is a skill I see as hovering on the edge of the endangered species list these days. To truly listen both requires presence and deepens presence; one must be present to listen and listening makes one more present.

As babies we live entirely in the present moment, there is only now and it is lived whole heartedly. Try telling a three year old they can have ice cream in one hour's time. To that child it will be a long, difficult and incomprehensible hour; they just want it now.

As children, we start to develop abilities to comprehend the passage of time and the nature of desire. As we grow, so our lives and brains grow increasingly complex. By five years old we are compelled to be in places we don't want to be and learn to be physically present while being emotionally and mentally absent.

After years of this we can actually find it difficult to be where we are, to gather all our attention into this moment. Add modern technology into the mix and our lives become virtual, two dimensional.

Listening anchors us in the here and now. Our minds are able to take our attention into the future or past with ease, but very little of our thinking is concerned with the present moment. If you listen to the thoughts in your head they are rarely about what is happening now and if they are it is often to compare the current experience with previous judgements.

Our emotions are generally taken up with attraction to or repulsion from another person or with dwelling upon past hurts or attachments. It is usually only our bodies that are here, so using the senses brings our attention back into the body.

Experiment — *in a moment stop reading and listen to your environment, if you are indoors, listen intently until you hear sounds from outside the room you are in. Observe what happens with you, maybe you calmed down, noticed your breathing or heard something you had not noticed. By noticing what is happening around us we also become more aware of ourselves as our level of presence rises and more of our attention is here.*

Listening is the first step in improvisation; listening to the audience, your fellow actors, director and to yourself. Actively listening also turns down the critical voice in the head that we all have. This is the self monitoring mechanism that we use to store the learning experiences which enable us to function in society. Initially it is programmed with useful information such as:

"Put your trousers on before you go to school"
"Don't challenge really big kids to a fight"
"Avoid fingers in light socket next time"
"Don't point at weird bloke on bus"
"Saying "thank you" results in more chocolate in the long run"

This memory bank also gets filled with not so useful messages such as,
"You are stupid/ selfish/ lazy/ greedy/ slow/ bad/ oversensitive/ insensitive/

pushy/ a pushover/ too loud/ too quiet/ shy/ show off" etc etc etc.

or "You are a slow learner"

"You idiot/ loser/ failure/ dimwit/ creep/ teacher's pet/ dunce"etc etc etc.

When we undertake any new and exciting endeavour this survival mechanism kicks in to keep us safe. Once again it is life or death and the messages loudly put us down right when we need support.

Listening to what is going on around us lowers the volume on this character and gives us the freedom to fly. After repeatedly going through this experience, the voice in the head sounds like a sad lonely stranger rather than the voice of God.

So if you are improvising or leading a group - then listen. If you get lost or overwhelmed - then listen. If scenes are flowing and going really well - then listen. You get the point.

Here's a story. I was leading a session with 30 very sharp people who were improvising for the first time. We were getting close to the end and were doing an exercise involving two people, working intensely together for 60 seconds, to improvise an advertisement for a product suggested by the audience. Everyone in the room had been except for the last pair. As they came up to the front, I noticed they were the only non-native English speakers in the room, and my useful inner voice quietly observed that this was an opportunity. I asked that they both did the exercise only in their native language, so we got to experience an advertisement for glow in the dark, solid footballs in a blend of German and Portuguese. It worked too.

Here's a result. The CEO of a medical supply company, let us call him Paul, attended an improvisation workshop and loved it. He forgot about the pressure of running a company and simply enjoyed himself. His own words about the experience were, "It fed my soul."

Next morning his secretary, let's call her Katy, who was a vital long term employee, reminded him that she was leaving early on Friday as she did every other Friday. This annoyed him a little, but feeling open and cheerful after the workshop, he asked Katy what she got up to every other Friday. She replied that she was taking a course in Reiki – a form of hands on healing. He was also trained in Reiki so they started to chat.

As the conversation progressed Katy showed him a sealed envelope on her desk. It was her resignation letter which she had intended to hand in at the end of the day. Taken aback, Paul asked her why and she replied that, as much as she enjoyed the job, she felt that he did not care about her and was not interested in her. (Most employees currently resign due to having a poor relationship with their manager.) Having listened, chatted, and been open to the moment, Paul was able to rejuvenate the relationship and retain a highly valued member of staff, someone he had seen as part of the family, but had not listened to. Katy stayed, and got a pay raise. Paul now listens to all his people and the company is thriving.

By listening we can discover possibilities that present themselves in the moment and make best use of our innate talents and the gifts that life offers.

The preceding story also leads us rather neatly into the next technique, which brings what we hear out onto the stage - that is - saying "Yes".

say yes

In improvising, effectively, we must engage with and suspend one of our most engrained programmes, which is the tendency to play it safe when facing new options and to say "No".

We are constantly compelled to make choices in an environment where we are bombarded with stimulation and advertising. We need to defend ourselves and screen out threats, exploitation and obligation.

Neuroscience suggests that much of the activity of the brain is used in determining what to screen out and ignore rather than what to notice, similar to the deflector shields in *Star Trek*. Enormous amounts of energy are involved in resisting perceived threats resulting in non presence.

Having been educated in school to avoid "mistakes", we become risk averse and it is always safer to say "No".

In companies, there is a clear perception of the need to innovate during these times of rapid change, but very few managers and CEOs want to be remembered as the guy who gave the thumbs up to today's equivalent of *New Coke*. So the messages are "Innovate but don't fail" and "Take risks but cover your arse".

In improvisation we have a safe arena – the stage upon which to try something new and different. It works when we say "Yes" and it all just grinds to a halt when we say "No". Improvisers are initially encouraged and later they are required to say "Yes" to whatever they are offered onstage, so when an improviser validates the emergent reality and adds to it, magic happens.

So, for example, if you are improvising onstage and your fellow actor says "Have an apple" you have many ways to say "yes" to this offer, such as,
"Thanks."
"Oh no I am allergic to Cox's Orange Pippins – it's the skin."
"I am so tired of your health nut agenda, always trying to fill me with fruit so I can't fit in a cheeseburger."

All the above are valid acceptances of the offer and reality that the other actor has an apple in their hand. Denying this would be to say something like, "That's not an apple, it's a hand grenade."

It is likely that the audience will laugh awkwardly at this point, but at what price? Your fellow actor is confused and their reality has been denied, while the audience does not know what is actually happening. We laugh at juxtaposition, when two things don't quite fit, but are in the same place. At this point you have damaged trust with your fellow actor and the audience and must work much harder even to get back to where you began. Just say "Yes" to the apple next time.

Experiment — *try this with a friend or colleague. One of you initiate a conversation about anything; it's handy to start with a preference or proposal e.g "I like ..." or "Let's go ..." The other responds with a sentence that begins "Yes, and ...". Then every subsequent sentence begins "Yes, and ...". Give it a shot and see what happens. Try starting your "Yes, and ..." response without having any idea how the sentence will end. If you get stuck just say "Yes, and ..." This is a classic improvisation exercise and the results are usually surprising, hilarious and/ or profound. Try it at a staff meeting.*

For some people it is difficult to say "Yes, and ..." to another person. It means letting go of control and security and trusting the other person will not exploit you while trusting yourself to come up with something.

Here's a story and another learning experience.

I was engaged to run an improvisation session for the change management team of a large bank. I had been told that as they were in change management, they were flexible, open to change and would love the session. As it turned out, the team was very fond of telling other people how to change and what to change, but none too keen to embrace even playing around with change themselves.

My plan for the session went out of the window and I decided to get them flowing with a rapid burst of "Yes, and ..." - a nice easy one.

There were two people in front of the room and about ten people watching.

One man, whom we will call Pete, could not begin more than one sentence with "Yes, and ...". Inevitably, he would start the next response "No, but ..." we worked on it with the support of the group. Pete had absolutely no idea he was doing this. The habit was so engrained that he honestly believed he was saying "Yes, and ..." while we could plainly hear "No, but ..." We worked at it, and after a few goes and different suggestions for a first sentence, Pete moved on to "No, and ...", then on to "Yes, but ...". This was progress of a kind. After some more work we got to the point where Pete was starting most sentences with "And yes..." which is close... but no cigar! We could go no further. Pete had come as far as he could that afternoon and to let go of that last bit of control was a step too far.

One of the benefits of improvisation is that getting into the habit onstage of saying "Yes" carries over into our lives and opens doors offstage as well. We become more willing to give something a go, to see what happens, rather than trying to think through the outcome before we make a move.

Once we have become more present by listening and saying "Yes" to the moment, we can exercise one more discipline to propel ourselves further into the magic – commitment.

COMMIT

You are onstage. The audience is watching, your fellow actor has presented an offer, an alternative temporary reality, you have said "Yes" and joined in – then what?

At this point the need for commitment arises.

In order to maintain the flow, to flourish in this brand new world that you are co-creating, it is essential to commit. To retract or play safe at this point invites disaster. It can all evaporate in a second if you don't believe in it even though your logical mind says it isn't true. There is nothing actually there, it is all made up. The inner critic is waiting to "protect" you from ridicule by telling you "This isn't working, you look stupid". Your reptilian brain is recognising that, not only are you outnumbered, but everyone is looking at you.

I chose the image of the Fool from the Tarot card deck for the cover of this book because he embodies the action an improviser takes again and again. That is, the empty handed step into the void. As he steps off the edge of the cliff the Fool is looking upwards for inspiration, not towards the ground or behind him. He steps out, carefree, and hopes for the best. Improvisers put themselves in situations where the only way out is in, the only way around is through, the only safety is in risk and there is nowhere to hide. There is no script to fall back on and no one to save them. Under these circumstances magic must happen. It doesn't always work; otherwise it would not be a risk.

The fear that most beginning improvisers express to me is that they will go blank and have nothing to say. My response is, that if they achieve this, they get an ovation because, at that moment, they are very present, with no thoughts, memories or plans operating.

Meditators practice for years so they can totally empty their minds and experience nothingness, but improvisers can stumble upon this experience when they least expect or want it – onstage in front of an audience! If you really want to empty your mind, step on stage without a script and try to think of something to say.

Having reframed the experience that improvisers fear, they are now free to leap into the unknown fully committed. There is tremendous power in commitment when we know the "what" i.e. the scene, without knowing the "how" i.e. the content or outcome.

In one of the Indiana Jones films, Indy must cross an abyss by stepping out onto a bridge that can only appear when someone is standing on it. In improvisation commitment conjures up the bridge as we step on it.

In the words of William Hutchinson Murray from his 1951 book entitled *The Scottish Himalayan Expedition,*
"Until one is committed, there is hesitancy, the chance to draw back.

Concerning all acts of initiative (and creation), there is one elementary truth, the ignorance of which kills countless ideas and splendid plans: that the moment one definitely commits oneself, then Providence moves too. All sorts of things occur to help one that would never otherwise have occurred. A whole stream of events issues from the decision, raising in one's favor all manner of unforeseen incidents and meetings and material assistance, which no man could have dreamed would have come his way. Whatever you can do, or dream you can do, begin it. Boldness has genius, power, and magic in it. Begin it now."

Experiment — *make a commitment to yourself to do something a little bit silly and out of the ordinary and then do it. One of my favourite ways of spreading a bit of fun is to say something wacky with a straight face and see how alive the other person becomes.*

Some sparkly moments I have created have been:

- Asking for a first class ticket on a bus

- Walking into a shop called *The Mobile Phone Repair Shop* and asking "Do you repair mobile phones?". The response was slack jawed amazement, pointing at the sign, then raucous laughter when the assistant realized I was kidding.

- Every time I go into my local fishmongers I ask him if he still sells fish. He is on to me now but still really enjoys the banter.

- I have haggled for train tickets, offered cash - no receipt needed and the results are hilarious; it makes the other person's day and gives them a story to tell at tea break.

Give it a go! The inner critic will try to stop you and your hands will sweat but, once you get a taste for turning ordinary transactions into harmless fun, it is hard to stop and life becomes more joyful. An ordinary moment becomes extraordinary and memorable because our attention is brought more into the present. This takes commitment because so much of our programming is designed to stop us doing or saying the wrong thing. Listening, Saying "Yes" and Committing are the basic tools we use to start improvising. After fifteen years, they are the tools I use to improvise both onstage and offstage. We always come back to the basics because they work. They are like a sword that you just keep sharpening.

In Act Two I will divulge the basic exercises that I use when teaching a group of people who are improvising for the first time. At my weekly class, which has regulars who have been attending for five years and have gone on to perform, we still use these exercises. When the Maydays get together to practice we still use these exercises. They continue to produce hilarity and profound learning and they always will.

Act Two

A DIY Guide to Basic Improvisation

Having ploughed through (or possibly skipped) Part One, we now move from talking about improvisation to the actual doing.

A principle I learned, and was delighted to put into practice, is the 70% rule, which comes from the martial art of Aikido. The idea is, that when we decide to do something new, we are tempted to give it 100%, believing this is the only way to make it happen. This is especially evident in New Year's resolutions, as shown when someone who is overweight resolves to take up running and lose weight. They set a goal of five miles per day and force their body to slog through the first few days or maybe a week, giving it 100%. Pretty soon their body will rebel and refuse to suffer any more, so the resolution goes out of the window, and there is no more running.

The 70% rule would have them run or even walk to 70% of their capacity, even if it is only a mile. The body feels OK and willing to do 70% the next day, so the capacity steadily builds until they can comfortably run five miles daily and may even look forward to it.

I recommend applying this principle to improvisation; don't push or try to get it right. Take your time, let it unfold, celebrate the wobbly moments and enjoy the ride. You will go further this way. Start slowly, be gentle and easy with yourself and everyone else and the journey will bring a lifetime of delight. Once you have a group of people, willing and able, who may be your team at work, family or a bunch of friends, then use this process as your guide until you are experienced enough to do it your way.

- **Set the Scene**

It is vital to establish an environment of safety, trust and support. It is impossible to spend too long doing this and also totally non-productive to do anything else until you have. There are certain points to communicate and reinforce which create an environment where people feel free to express.

Having recently passed my UK driving test on the third go, my personal learning from the many driving lessons I took was that, a good improv teacher is like a driving instructor. The student has the wheel, you are showing them how and they are steering but you have your own brake and clutch. This means the student is driving but you can stop if they are steering at a wall and accelerating. They have the thrill and experience of driving while you keep them safe.

During the set up and throughout the session repeat these three messages (the number three shows up a lot in comedy).

- **It is impossible to do improvisation wrong.**

Improvisation is whatever you make in the moment. Obviously, there is no physical violence permitted, but whatever else you come out with is just fine. The underlying message here is to the reptilian brain and says - "You will not be judged, ostracized, killed or eaten" because there is no such thing as a wrong reply or bad line. There are guidelines which help the flow, but if the student keeps saying "No" when the guideline is to say "Yes", that is perfect.

At a meta level, as a facilitator, you must have your "Yes" to their "No" and engage with them where they are in that moment. It is impossible to do improvisation wrong - there, I said it again, and I will say it dozens of times in a 90 minutes session. Many people do not hear it until the fifteenth time because the reptilian brain isn't letting it penetrate the neocortex. Once this has gone in and you are certain that all the group have heard it - they may even be saying it to each other - then say it again because they will forget. So will you if that same person says "No" again! It is impossible to do this wrong.

• **There is no need to be quick, clever or funny in order to do this.**

In fact trying to do so will make it harder for you to relax and collaborate. The underlying message here is to the mammalian brain and is saying, "You are part of the group, you are in, you do not need to pass a test to be included, you have support."

Be alert for the person, let's call them Jen, who says something like, "I'm in the right place then, because I'm a bit slow/ unfunny/ thick/ an accountant etc." This is their inner critic speaking out loud. We met this character in part one, in the chapter on listening. It is a positive sign that they have verbalized this because it means that, while they are nervous, they feel safe enough to reveal this. Give them a smile, resist the urge to offer any contradiction and mentally flag up Jen in your mind. Later on in the session, as soon as Jen comes out with something even remotely funny, then ruthlessly single her out for some positive attention in front of the whole group. Say something like

"Jen, that was spot on, brilliant" then compound the moment by turning to the group and saying "Wasn't that great everyone!" At that moment, having previously emerged in public, Jen's inner critic is outnumbered and outvoted. Indeed, it may well be mortally wounded by this experience and never be able to hold her back again. We all have a virtual reality based picture of ourselves and improv can shatter that distorting mirror in an instant.

- **We Have a Set of Guidelines**

We usually want to do things well, follow the programme and get it right. Let your group know that there are tried and tested guidelines for improvisation, simple and effective techniques which they will learn together as they go, just like the rules to a game.

No acting experience is necessary and there will not be any Oscars handed out at the end. If the goal is just to be who they are, however they are in the moment and to express, engage and enjoy then they can let go of trying to follow some imaginary agenda. If the structure is in place and they are safe and the structure is nice and loose then they can relax into it.

The underlying message here is to the neocortex, "There is a process to follow which doesn't really need much effort or planning if you want to just find the appropriate word now and then that would help." The neocortex can then adopt a role and relish the flow of language, situations and ideas that emerges. Depending on the nature and composition of the group, setting the scene may take from one minute to twenty minutes. If it is taking longer than twenty minutes either you are working with the wrong group for improv or you are floundering – commit! It is impossible to do this wrong. Having set the scene, and reassured all three brains of all the participants, including yourself of course, it is good to start off with something everyone does together. This raises the energy level in the room and gets the nervous types on board and engaged with everyone.

Whole Group Games

Hello, As If

This is one of my favourite warm ups. Get everyone to wander around the room randomly and tell them they only need one word for this exercise.

Instruction 1: When they make eye contact with someone say "Hello" to them, just hello, nothing else and then walk on and repeat this with someone else. Let this run for a minute or two unless they are really loving it.

Instruction 2: Ask them to keep wandering but this time when they make eye contact to say "Hello" as if they are embarrassed, then walk on and repeat. Again let this continue while the energy is high.

Instruction 3: As above but keep changing the "as if" - so "Hello" as if they are hyperactive, bored, seductive, constipated, French, broke etc.

Instruction 4: Tell them you are going to give them one more "as if" suggestion which they will use, then three group members will come up with their own "as ifs" which everyone must use, one after the other.

Likely outcomes: laughter, feeling of relief from shy ones, those who made suggestions will feel validated and heard, high energy level in the room, enthusiasm, connections between people, loads of good stuff.

Flag Up: They are doing great, this is how improv works, what fun this is, it's impossible to do this wrong, and perhaps they want more. Once the group is up and moving the next one works a treat with up to 30 people.

Zip Zap Boing

Get everyone in a circle so they can all see each other. Join the circle and if no one stands near you make a joke about that.

Instruction 1: Demonstrate by swiftly pointing at the person to your left with both index fingers and saying "Zip" loudly and with enthusiasm. Invite them to do the same to the person to their left and continue this process around the room.

Once it gets back to you, wait a beat and say, "This time send it around as fast as you can"

Let it go round a few times encouraging greater speed.

Instruction 2: When it gets back to you, stop and add another option, when the "Zip" reaches them they can say "Zip" and send it on or look at the person who zipped them, raise both hands and say "Boing" which bounces it back the way it came. Tell them they can only "Boing" a "Zip" and immediately send a "Zip" fast and loud.

Inevitably chaos will occur, someone will "Boing" a "Boing" and everyone will laugh, ask the group why they are laughing and reinforce "It is impossible to do this wrong" because the, so called, mistakes are the best bit! Keep it going as fast as possible until they get reasonably competent.

Instruction 3: Add a further twist. When the "Zip" comes to them they can "Zip" it along, "Boing" it back or they can make eye contact with anyone in the circle, clap and say "Zap" which sends it to that person. They can only "Boing" a "Zip".

The tension really rises, so, send a "Zip" loud and fast and wait for the chaos. Enjoy the laughter and celebrate the mistakes, of which there will be many. Some people totally panic when it gets to them and say "Bbbip" or "Zoing". If that happens, then celebrate it, and thank them for their creative response. Reinforce that it is impossible to do this wrong and that the mistakes are by far the best part. How boring would it be to have a group that could zip, zap and boing flawlessly on demand? It would be no fun at all, and how lucky we are to be in a group so creatively inspired that they can't get round the circle once without a whole new innovative technique being discovered!

Outcomes: Group feels safer and more energised and bonded. The message that it is impossible to do this wrong is being reinforced. The mistakes are being celebrated and those who are making mistakes are receiving praise and positive feedback from the big scary facilitator and the group. We are not in Kansas anymore; there is some serious deprogramming of the education software that lurks inside the participants taking place.

Flag Up: Both during and afterwards – that they are doing really well, it's fun, and mistakes are the best bit. Also reinforce that they can do this exercise in any meeting from now on. Ask them to notice what inner talk went on during this process and offer or elicit from them possible examples:

"You are getting it wrong."
"Just keep zipping and you can't fail."
"I can do this faster than so and so."
"I'm going to boing my colleague and trip them up."

It can be a real relief for people to realise that we all have similar messages running in our heads and that they don't have to rule our lives if we choose otherwise.

So, by now the whole group is buzzing and hopefully curious about what comes next. If the group is too large for zip,.zap, boing then you can use the next game to create similar effects or later on, after a break to raise the energy levels.

Point and Call

This one works brilliantly with a large group and opens the mind to see and think differently. It also has an element of frustration, which is useful to address as it is something we tend to avoid, yet is often a part of the process of change and growth.

Instruction 1: Demonstrate walking around the room while pointing at and naming what you choose i.e. point at the wall with your left hand and shout "wall" then point at a door with your right hand and shout "door" and so on. Do it fast and encourage them to point then call, rather than looking at an object, then pointing at it then naming it. Show them that you point, then look, then name. It is a process of discovery. When you demonstrate, do it so fast that you point, look and say "Don't know" then point elsewhere. This gives permission to fail and put discovery before getting it right. Have them start.

Instruction 2: Tell them they are doing well and then tell them that, this time when they point, they are to shout out any word except the actual name of the object or person. Demonstrate by pointing and naming as fast as you can until you lose it, point at something and go "Aaaah!" Be absurd, point at the wall and say "elephant" then point at a desk and say "Reginald Maudling". Again you set the tone and give permission to fail. Set them loose to have a go.

Instruction 3: Demonstrate this version. When you point at the first object say nothing. When you point at the next object call out the previous object and so on. So, if the first object you point at is a vase, say nothing, then point at a fire extinguisher and say "vase", then point at a chair and say "fire extinguisher" and so on. Keep going, fast as you can, alternating hands until you lose it. It won't take long! Then turn them loose to have a go.

Outcomes: Laughter, frustration, chaos, determination, new neural pathways forming, creative thinking, happy bewilderment.

Flag Up: They are doing really well; it's impossible to do this wrong; this one is supposed to be frustrating; frustration means you are striving for more. Comment on the effort and concentration in the room. If you observed someone who seems really confident moving in slow motion during the third part, ask if you can impersonate them for those who missed it. They normally love it, if they don't take themselves too seriously, and you have also demonstrated your own incompetence in this realm. Ask them what they noticed happening inside themselves. Did they give up? Get angry? Were they competitive? Did they enjoy it although it was a big mess? All responses are good ones. If they want to practice this later encourage them not to do it in public!

At this point the group will be open and enthusiastic. As a facilitator you have not taken yourself too seriously yet are moving things along. There is a feeling of trust, safety and enthusiasm in the room. So, it's time to turn it up a notch. Thus far they have improvised as a group and we are now moving into improvising onstage. For many people this is an intimidating prospect, because we have disempowered ourselves and set actors and performers up on pedestals, when actually, in the words of John Gielgud, "Theatre is just a bunch of people shouting at each other onstage."

At the same time, in life, we are expected to interact effectively with other people, often without any training or preparation in being aware of how we come across. The stage can be a truly magical place where we can try out different ways of being and then choose to carry those new ways into our offstage lives. We can raise our awareness of ourselves and explore options in a safe environment – if it is safe.

It is useful to demystify the stage at this point. It is a special place but it is open to anyone willing to step upon it. The next step for the participants is onto the stage.

Stand and Deliver

This is one of the very few improvisation exercises that I invented from scratch.

The world of improvisation is a totally open source environment where people copy, adapt, tinker, steal and plagiarise constantly and it is all the better for it. When something works, improvisers use it. When other improvisers see it working, they use it themselves and on it goes. Bits get dropped, added, lost, forgotten, rearranged and cross bred in the process; it's a lot like nature. The strong stuff survives, flourishes and reproduces.

When I work with business owners I am, occasionally, asked what steps I take to protect my intellectual property and they are usually horrified when I cheerily reply, "None at all". In fact I hope people do "steal" my work. If I know who invented a particular exercise I will give them credit when I use it and if people do the same for me that's nice. I have benefited massively from the contributions of improvisers I will never meet and get a chance to thank. If I can add a little to the mix then I am fortunate enough to be able to give something back in gratitude. I believe collaboration is one of the finest acts of humanity and improvisation is a great example of the benefits of generosity. So, to the exercise. Like so many it looks flat on paper but springs to life onstage.

Instruction 1: Announce to the group that they are about to be trained in stagecraft. With tongue firmly in cheek, play up the strenuous challenges involved and propose that each of them spends several seconds in intensive training.

This is a four step process which each person will go through. There will be a batch of people, say 4 or 5 to the side of the stage. Once the audience has suggested a short sentence each person in turn will go through this process:

- They will stand solo, centre stage facing the audience.
- They will deliver the sentence that the audience has given them.
- The audience will then applaud - they will stand while this happens.
- When the applause ends they return to their seat.

Each one of the batch will in turn go through this process delivering the same line. Another batch will then come to the stage, the audience will give a suggestion which could be a single word, a cliché, a number or just about anything. The four step process is repeated with this batch and so on until everyone in the room has had a go. Let them know that the aim is not a theatrical presentation, it is impossible to do it wrong and that the group is on their side. Reading this, I am fairly sure, dear reader, you think it sounds rubbish. However I always use this one and have seen people helpless with laughter, shaking with sheer terror, giving it their all and having huge triumphs. People have created uproarious laughter, simply by saying the number 27 with pathos or panache. It is not the words that count, but what people bring to the process, and what they bring is their emotion, passion and creative genius. To stand, solo on stage, before an audience, with just a word or two to deliver is an act of courage. Logically, it is not a big deal, but it feels significant, because one is in sharp focus when the attention of a group of people is concentrated and waiting for you to deliver. When the applause comes, that in itself is a highly charged moment and brings up all kinds of issues. Most people leave the stage during the applause because it is just too

uncomfortable to receive that much positive attention. Some actually run
squealing to their seats. The inner critic gets to have the volume turned up
and chips in with all kinds of put downs and disaster scenarios.

One reaction that I often catch, in the moment, is when someone delivers a
line in a way that the group just loves and enjoys. The next person in line will
look at me and say "How am I going to follow that?" If the group is open to
learning at that point, I will pounce and dissect the situation. One person has
created a moment of magic, but the next person is comparing the
contribution they imagine they are about to make with the moment that just
happened. Strictly speaking neither of those moments exist except as images in
the mind – one from the immediate past and one from an imagined
immediate future. The only purpose the mind is using these images for is to
undermine the person by subtly saying, "What you are about to do is not as
good as that person just did." We examine this dynamic and I encourage the
person to return to the present where neither image exists and they are free
from the *help* of the mind.

There is no credit or debit in improvisation; it all takes place in the here and
now. A performer can have a moment of genius and then fall flat on their face
a second later. Conversely, you may absolutely die onstage many times but, if
you let go and return to the present moment, you have every opportunity for
pure inspired magic to unfold. This is part of what makes improvisation so
liberating and life-affirming; one has the option to continually renew ones
connection with the here and now.

Outcomes: Each person has taken a risk and come out the other side; the group has bonded further through a shared ordeal - they have trodden the boards and are still alive and breathing. There is much learning here around attention, giving and receiving, self talk, praise, success and the virtual reality we can live in.

Flag Up: They are doing great and they have just become trained actors! They have successfully taken a shared risk. Draw attention to the quiet ones who have blossomed before our eyes, the level of presence that is in the room, the power of letting go of expectation or regret. If someone has left the stage saying, "That was awful" while the audience applauded wildly, then talk about how our self talk does not match outside reality. Some will stubbornly cling to the idea that they are genuinely rubbish at this point - that changes as we go on.

From actor to improviser is but a short step. They simply use the same stagecraft and commitment without a script. It's time for some scenes.

It is up to you as facilitator, when you bring in the three golden guidelines,

- Listen.
- Say, "Yes".
- Commit.

You may want to keep things moving at this point or offer some structure. It's your call. If you do want to introduce the guidelines it's good to make some of the learning experiential. I always talk about listening and then have them do a simple, yet fiendishly difficult, listening exercise as follows.

Let them know they are going to be counting from one to twenty in order, one number at a time. This is very valuable for raising group awareness on all levels.

You will kick off by saying "One" and then one of the group should say "Two". Then another of them will say "Three" and so on until they get to twenty. The twist is that if two people say the same number they start again at "One".

There is no cheating allowed e.g. pointing at the next person, standing up before you say a number, going in order round the room etc – I've seen them all! You get to define cheating as taking away the benefit of the exercise. This really brings people into the present. You can feel the atmosphere change in the room as they get more involved in seeing how to pull this one off successfully. If the group get to twenty after a few goes they tend to go nuts. It's worth spending a few moments talking about the experience, as some people can actually physically sense when it is their turn to speak. There are some interesting conversations about moments where someone knows a certain number is theirs and also how important it is to not say a number. People can really get intrigued by the potential benefits of deep listening.

Next, let your group know that when they listen onstage, with that sort of focus, they will have all the resources they need to improvise well. Talk about the power of just saying "yes" onstage. Remind them that a scene is a temporary reality and if they can just go with it, something magic can happen and it's impossible to do it wrong anyway. Once they have listened and said "Yes", then the commitment will fuel a triumphant scene. It works like a mathematical formula if they stick to all three guidelines. If they find they can't do all three and it all falls apart then we all laugh and it doesn't matter anyway, because as always, it is impossible to do it wrong.

If the guideline is to listen and someone doesn't listen, then that too is great, because that is what is happening in the moment. If they say "No" and don't commit then that is the scene and it is also perfect because that is what is happening in the moment. It is impossible to do this wrong!

As facilitator of an improv session you give people the guidelines, support in using them and total open hearted permission to fail as often and as badly as they wish. Perversely, the more honestly you can do this then the better it works. If you should find yourself judging participants, or feeling frustrated with someone who won't listen and you are telling yourself you are a crap facilitator, that's great too. Because that is what is happening in this moment, and the next moment will be different. It may even get worse, which is perfect, because that is what is happening in that moment and it is impossible to do this wrong. Apply the 70% rule, be gentle with yourself and enjoy the ride.

Are you ready for some scenes?

Basic Scenes

It is best to start with small steps. Build the confidence and enthusiasm of the group and then add complexity. Remember that you are the driving instructor with your own brake and clutch. Stop the movement and slip the session into neutral when you wish, then get it going again. The next game I learned from the fabulous Lorenzo Aragon, when we worked together in Essential Theatre Playback Company of Arizona. It quickly allows beginners to gain confidence in interacting and creates much laughter and enables experienced improvisers to get into the zone and bond before a show or rehearsal.

Three Line Scene

Instruction 1: Get four people onstage or up in front of the room. Explain that they are going to do some three line scenes which are the building blocks of improvisation. These are the world's shortest scenes - just two actors with three lines between them. Let's call them actor A and actor B.

Actor A says the first line, and actor B responds with a related line then actor A responds with the third. End of scene.

Remind them that it is impossible to do this wrong because if they should go crazy, lose count, get carried away and do four lines by mistake, then we have got an extra line for free. If they are laughing too hard to deliver the third line, which does happen, that is fine too.

Demonstrate this with actor A. Start the first scene yourself, then let them start the next scene. Let them know they are doing well and get the audience to applaud them after each scene. Let them know that it is absolutely fine to go blank in this one and if it happens they should simply say, "I don't know what to say."

Demonstrate this scenario too, with one of the actors. Tell them you are going to do a few scenes together, that you will do the first line and their line is always, "I don't know what to say." Then throw a few first lines at them, such as,
" I want to marry you."
"You are under arrest."
"That's my seat." And so on.

They respond with "I don't know what to say" each time and the audience gets to relax. Many first time improvisers are terrified of not having a response.

You have now both given them permission to fail and reinforced that it is impossible to do this wrong. Good!

So you have four actors on stage, actors A, B, C and D in a line facing the audience, ready to go. Instruct actor A to do a three line scene with actor B. Immediately have actor B do a three line scene with actor C and so on. This means each actor is doing two scenes back to back and has no time to plan in between them. After C and D do a scene, have actor D and actor A do one – they weren't expecting that! Repeat this a few times. Have the audience applaud the first four actors as they leave the stage. It looks flat on paper, but is rich onstage. I still start every weekly drop in class with this one and continually add refinements, sharpening the sword.

Instruction 2: Focus all the attention on the bits that worked. If someone delivers a great line and gets a huge laugh then repeat the line. The audience will laugh again and the actor will feel heard and validated. Bring four more actors to the stage. You are now going to repeat the process and add refinements. Have the actors go down the line once doing scenes, then add a restriction. Instruct them to avoid asking questions. Making a statement adds information for the other actor to build on, whilst asking a question makes the other actor do most of the work. Inevitably the next batch of scenes will be full of questions; this is called Sod's Law. The audience will be laughing, the actors will be happily frustrated, so slip it into neutral, by reminding them it is "impossible to do this wrong". The instruction is to avoid questions, but the actors keep asking questions, so the audience is having fun. The mistakes are the best bit!

Continue, and raise the stakes by challenging them to do four three line scenes in a row without a single question. If they achieve this, they get a huge round of applause and get to sit down. If they don't achieve this, they get a huge round of applause and get to sit down.

We always make a profit in improvisation if we set the scene well. Follow the guidelines and they will work like a mathematical formula to create compelling, hilarious drama. If you attempt to follow the guidelines and it just doesn't happen, then it is even funnier.

Nancy Howland Walker is a superb teacher of improvised song, and she says that when you walk onto a stage in front of an audience your IQ immediately drops 50 points. If participants are intrigued and wonder why they cannot do three lines without asking a question I always quote this statistic as applying to myself.

Instruction 3: The participants now have a device to play with – the three line scene. As a facilitator you can provide new input and applications for this device. Bring four more actors to the stage and have them do a series of three line scenes avoiding questions. They will often be able to do this more easily than the previous batch. This is a good time to mention the concept of the "group mind", the idea that a group of people can learn through, and benefit from, the experience of other members of the group.

Let them know that part of your role as facilitator is to continually raise the bar, to add complexity, so the group learning is continually expanding and that, as soon as they are becoming competent at an exercise, you will make it more challenging. The goal is not to get it right or do it well. The purpose is to simply be yourself in the moment; sweating, laughing, frustrated, applauding, embarrassed, scared, regretful, triumphant, astonished, fumbling or annoyed. It's all just fine. To access the inner magic we ride this roller coaster together. We have permission to fail, as we are wrestling with something brand new and challenging, but sometimes, for a moment, we are in the zone. As soon as we congratulate ourselves or tell ourselves to try harder, we lose it again. We find something that worked in a scene, do it again in the next scene, and it doesn't work. Welcome to the wacky world of improvisation.

So, again add complexity. This time have the batch of actors start each three line scene by giving the other actor a title such as Reverend, Admiral, Jeeves, Doctor etc. Encourage the other actor to embody that title by changing their physicality. There is no wrong response, so if the first actor says, "Your Majesty the ambassador has arrived", the other actor may embody regality by standing erect and sniffing, or they may do it by picking their nose. It doesn't matter what the choice is, as long as they make one. Giving a title to someone allows them to be someone else for a moment.

Here's a list of ways you can add twists to these scenes:

- First line gives the other actor a different name, a simple but liberating twist.

- First line begins in the middle of a sentence.

- First line begins with "you".

- First line is boring, second line is an emotional over-reaction.

- First line and first line only is a line from a song, spoken not sung.

- First line is a cliché from advertising.

There are many ways to add productive twists to this simple exercise.

Outcomes: Laughter, challenge to habitual thinking, confidence and bonding of group goes up, desire to continue increases.

Flag Up: Validate the shy ones who have had victories. Remind them that if you can do a three line scene you can do any improvisation. Notice how they wanted to keep going after three lines, how funny we are when we are just being ourselves. It's impossible to do this wrong.

Business Applications: The opening of this channel of thinking and responding has inspired many companies to apply the learning to interviews, client meetings, brainstorming sessions, presentations and staff training.

1 to 20

This exercise is simple, yet highly engaging and has enthralled many groups to the point where they have been absolutely spellbound and astonished at what emerges.

It is worth a few words about physical embodiment at this point. We communicate our inner state quite clearly with our bodies, so if we try to cover up what is showing on the surface, that will also be visible to other people. When our verbal, physical and emotional expression are congruent, then we are communicating effectively. When they are not congruent any audience will sense and feel this, even if they cannot put their discomfort into words. This exercise looks at physical expression and is simple in structure and rich in content.

Instruction 1: Bring a chair to the front of the room. Let the audience know that this scene involves three actors but they don't need to come up with any words.

There will be two actors onstage and one off to the side, in the wings, where we agree that they cannot be seen. The two actors onstage are going to have a dialogue. The chair is there as a prop, so they may sit on it, lean on it or ignore it. The scene is not about the chair and it stays on the floor at all times. The twist is that the actors speak in numbers from 1 to 20 in order, so if the first actor says 1,2,3,4 then the second actor replies, for example, 5, 6... and so on back and forth. The actors offstage are observing the scene and at some point, when they feel compelled to do so, will enter the scene and say the next number or numbers in the sequence. (Refer back to the listening exercise earlier when some people could sense which number was theirs and when to speak it out.) The other actors respond, dialogue continues until they get to 20 and then it is over.

Have them do one run through and then bring three more actors to the stage.

Instruction 2: Once the group see the structure, then encourage the actors to take their time in the scene, have eye contact and get a sense of their relationship. Have them both react to the entrance of the third actor, let it affect them. Are they happy to see this person arrive? Embarrassed? Relieved? Caught in the act?

Keep doing these scenes, the audience will start finding stories and characters. For example, there may be a scene presented where most of the group felt it was siblings on stage and then Dad arrived. Remind them of group mind and how powerful our physical communication can be. Explore the dynamics at play. The initial two actors have a relationship, when the third actor arrives, he/she is a catalyst and changes the situation just by entering. This is the interloper that we see in sit coms.

Remind everyone again that it is impossible to do this wrong. If someone is nervous about this scene and decides to wait in the wings until the other two get to 19 then run on yourself, say "20" and run off again. This is great, because by their reaction he/she has found a creative way to take part!

Instruction 3: Once most of the group has taken a turn at this you have an ace up your sleeve. If the group is small in number, then encourage everyone try both roles i.e. onstage role and offstage interloper. When you see a particularly juicy performance, with lots of movement and emotion, step in just after they get to 20. Ask the actors to return to their original positions and announce that, as the scene was so good, they are going to repeat it but, this time, they will replace the numbers with dialogue so we find out what they were saying. Have them start immediately, before doubt or panic get too deep. It always works and everyone is amazed.

If there are some people who are yet to have a turn, tell them that this is the only scene with words in and they will be back to just the numbers. Otherwise they will be thinking of dialogue while they do the numbers and it won't flow.

Outcomes: Laughter galore, amazement that it comes together; awareness of the effectiveness of physical communication and interpersonal dynamics. Actors and audience get so involved that they want to continue past 20.

Flag Up: Communication without words; group mind; timing; allowing yourself to be affected by the interloper; stepping into the unknown and actually flourishing; adding a level of complexity i.e. the dialogue and being able to create compelling drama from basis of movement.

Business Benefits: Importance of congruency in communications; power of non verbal expression; timing and reactions during meetings; influencing situations; coping with the unexpected; tapping into inner resources to deal with unexpected change or pressure.

We can take the spirit and dynamic nature of 1 to 20 into the next exercise.

Blank Family

This is one of my favourites and it's great fun for the audience, while building complexity and level of risk. I learned this from the late great Louis Anthony Russo. Thanks Lou.

Instruction 1: Place two chairs, centre stage, facing diagonally inwards. Take four actors, with two sitting on the chairs, and two offstage, one each side of the stage. This is a classic sit-com format. The chairs represent a couch in a living room, and there is a TV facing the couch. On the couch sit Mum and Dad, while offstage to one side them is their offspring, whilst offstage on the other side is the interloper.

The audience will fill in the "blank" of the title and give a suggestion of an attitude or condition of life e.g. uptight, absurdly rich, angry, jealous etc. Parents will embody that suggestion as completely as possible so everything in the environment, their conversation, what is on the TV, etc will reflect and amplify this.

For example, if the suggestion is "depressed" they could be watching *The Seventh Seal* on TV, eating beans from a tin, slumped on the couch and so on. Everything that occurs will increase their depression. Once this is established, their offspring will enter and add fuel to the fire. He may be looking for his Prozac, wearing Goth attire, speaking in monosyllables. Their dialogue will be on depressing subjects and make them more depressed. An audience loves to see this energy building, the actors are saying "Yes and ..." to massive downward depression.

Meanwhile, the interloper has a challenge. It is their role to find a way to embody the antitheses of everything onstage. They can do this in any number of ways, but mentally they are searching for a way to become the polar opposite of depression.

It may be by simply being hyper and positive or by picking an event or famous person who would be iconic of this.

Once the scene is established and the attitude is permeating the whole stage, then the interloper rings the doorbell, which may sound like the Death March or something equally miserable. The family is, of course, really depressed by having a visitor. The offspring opens the door, and the interloper enters the room, takes centre stage and announces,

"Hi, I've just moved in next door. I'm Tony Robbins!!!" or
"I'm here to let you know you have won the lottery!!!" or
"I'm here to tell you the good news about Jesus!!!" you get the picture.

The scene ends with the family frozen looking at the interloper.

Instruction 2: Once they have done one or two of these, then start to tinker. Have the family take longer to build the atmosphere and add more details to colour the scene. Ask for more subtle suggestions like regretful or conscientious. Have everyone take a turn at doing this and if the group is small have people play different roles to try them out. If someone in the audience has an inspired idea for an interloper, then re-run the end of the scene. Some families can have multiple interlopers show up. Audiences love repetition, especially if there is a different twist coming at the end.

Outcomes: Laughter galore; creative thinking; stretching to find interloper offers; understanding of the innate structure and nature of comedy and a sense of building tension together.

Flag Up: The joy of it; how much the interloper has to sweat; how well they are doing; the complexity of what they are creating together; group mind on the interloper possibilities – you often hear "I thought that too."

Business Benefits: Often a profound awareness of how an organisation creates a culture in the same way as the family creates the atmosphere. This leads to reflection on whether they have created the culture they really want and to questioning how the interloper gets treated in their company. Everything attracts its opposite sooner or later – I know quite a few peace activists who are very angry people!

The experience of creating a culture onstage, through choice, can have a deep impact on a company and lead to significant change. I have worked with a large mobile phone company in the UK which has put improvisation principle into practice and one is required to Listen, Say Yes and Commit at strategy meetings.

Home Shopping

This is another big favourite with many of the companies that I have worked with for reasons which will become apparent. It is based on a very specific form of television advertising – the infomercial. This is a programme which presents items for sale over a much longer time frame than an advert. There are even infomercial channels devoted to just one product line such as jewellery. The format is quite often that of a couple of people chatting about the item for sale in a friendly, personal manner while a band across the bottom of the screen displays the price, the number to call and how many of the items are still available. This is a highly successful format and the presenters are using the skills that improvisers use. They listen to each other, agree and keep going for hours. We use our own take on this to respond quickly and positively to audience suggestion and to collaborate closely onstage.

Instruction 1: Place two actors onstage and ask the audience to raise their hands if they have watched infomercials on TV. Men are often particularly reluctant to admit this. It's also fun to ask if people have bought anything and, if so, what item. Let the actors know that they are to present a sixty second infomercial. You will time them and the audience will suggest the item to be sold. Ask for an item, then add complexity so, if you get a toaster, ask what other features it has, so the audience may suggest it has satellite navigation. Then ask for another feature which no other toaster has, so they may say it's made of rubber and plays music.

At this point the audience is salivating with expectation and the actors are deeply traumatised and overwhelmed. No one believes they can pull this off successfully. Turn to the actors with your watch in your hand and sternly remind them to Listen, Say "Yes" and Commit. Repeat the features of the item in bite sized chunks. "So you are selling us a rubber toaster with sat nav that plays music. Action!" With the time pressure, task in hand and the last thing they heard being the information they need, they launch right in. Stop them around the sixty second mark - a bit earlier if they get a huge laugh, or a bit later if they are mid sentence.

Instruction 2: Tell the first pair they did well, then repeat the high points and invite the next pair onstage. Now you can tune up as you go, by inviting the actors to give each other different names during the scene. Tell them they know everything about this item and that they love it! Instruct them to be holding one, wearing one or have one right there in front of them, so it seems more real. Encourage them to repeat what the other actor just said, especially if they have no idea what to say. Coach them to focus on the benefits of the item more than the features.

You can change the nature of the item to fit your audience. You could ask for a new coaching method, e.g. a pitch for a movie, a brand new religion, a political party etc. Get another wacky item suggested by the audience and repeat the process until everyone has had a go.

Outcomes: Laughter galore; a realisation at how long sixty seconds can be when we are present and engaged in the moment; hugely innovative thinking and genius responses when under stress.

Flag Up: They are doing well; revisit the high points; validate those who have really stretched and blossomed; the power of suggestion – although you know, logically, that the item did not exist, did you find yourself wanting one?

Business Benefits: The shocking realisation that companies design and offer products and services, and focus on selling the features, when the customer is actually buying the benefits. This is not a theoretical learning. The group will realise it has just been demonstrated and astute business leaders will make the connection. Many companies use this technique internally to "sell" ideas and projects. It is a great brainstorming tool.

Having succeeded in embracing audience suggestions and immediately creating short, focussed magical scenes you may want to enjoy a bit of silliness that guarantees everyone gets to celebrate making mistakes.

Questions Only

This is a different format and has a slightly different purpose from the previous ones. It is an impossible task, which the actors do their utmost to succeed in and it just doesn't happen. The joy is in the tripping up and being happy to do so.

Instruction 1: With two actors onstage the audience will suggest a location, and the actors begin their scene in that location. The twist is, they are only allowed to speak in questions, hence the title. As soon as they make a statement or go blank the audience gleefully shouts "Get off!" and the actor who made the statement leaves the stage and another actor comes on. The actor that stayed remains in the same character in the same location and immediately asks the arriving actor a question. The process continues until everyone has had a go. Some groups want to go around twice, because they think they will do better the second time around. Encourage the actors to play obvious, recognisable characters who fit the location as this makes it more satisfying to watch and join. Counsellors often do really well at this, but don't be afraid to disallow repetition or hesitation.

Outcome: Laughter galore, and a certain piquant frustration - especially when someone watches a few people go before them, and convinces themselves that the actors are faking how hard it is, that they will do much better when it's their turn. They don't. I have seen people play this one many times and never get beyond their first word.

Flag Up: The sheer silliness of it; the competitiveness that arises even though they know it's silly; the joy of it; how earlier on, in three line scenes, no one could avoid asking questions and now, no one can come up with one. Sod's Law again.

Business Benefits: The realisation of how asking a question compels the other person to answer and the value of letting go of the unimportant details.

A bit more silliness next, then we are going to bring it all together...

Worst Thing

A more recent addition to my bag of tricks, this is light and simple, yet strangely liberating.

Instruction 1: Four actors are onstage, in a line, facing the audience. The audience will suggest an event or situation. Each actor in turn, as soon as he/she gets the impulse, will take a step forward, and say or do the worst possible thing they could do or say under the circumstances. Everyone will have a turn, so we will see four worst things for each event.

Give them two more suggestions (three is magic in comedy) then bring another batch of four actors onstage. Repeat until everyone has had a turn.

Outcomes: Loads of laughs; a sense of freedom through having been naughty; surprises at who came out with what; highly creative thinking once the obvious moves have been made.

Flag Up: They did fantastically; thinking outside the norm; element of risk; courage to step out of one's comfort zone.

Business Benefits: Breaking unspoken taboos in a safe setting; supporting maverick viewpoints; a bit of catharsis; useful messages that are typically suppressed or marginalised; considering different or unusual methods

Bringing it all together

Let's see if we can bring it all to a close by weaving together all that we have learned and experienced in a fast paced, complex, challenging exercise which would have been well outside of the capability of the group when the session started.

The Henry

I am indebted to Michael Gellman from Chicago, who invented this form and taught it in London a few years ago. He was asked to name it, so he called it *Henry*. The structure is simple yet uses all the techniques we have been exploring. The results can be funny, tragic, absurd and profound all at the same time.

Instruction 1: Place four chairs in a row onstage, facing the audience with one actor in each chair. Let us call them actor A, B, C and D.

The audience suggests the name of a village in which all four actors live and know each other. Each pair of actors A and B, B and C, C and D, and D and A are given a location in the village by the audience. Have the actors remind the audience of their locations (so that they remember themselves!) They will play the same character in both of their locations.

So, if A and B are in the pub and B and C are at the gym, and B has decided he is a farmer then B will be a farmer in the pub with A and the same farmer in the gym with C. The procedure is as follows – Actor A and actor B stand and do a 30 second scene (scene 1) in their location.

You time them and call "Next" after 30 seconds. Actor A sits down, Actor B remains standing and actor C immediately stands so that B and C then do a 30 second scene (scene 2) in their location. Call "Next" after 30 seconds and actor B sits down as Actor D stands and does a 30 second scene (scene 3) with C. Repeat "Next" so C sits, and D does a scene (scene 4) with A. The process repeats for a total of three times, which is twelve scenes for each "village". Somehow, if the actors have remembered even a fraction of what they have learned, this will all come together and create a drama with interlocking storylines, plots, subplots, surprise discoveries, love affairs and more. All of this happens in six minutes, improvised, on the spot, by people who have never done it before. I have had the pleasure of seeing the *Henry* work superbly hundreds of times and I continue to be thrilled by what comes out every single time.

Outcomes: Laughs galore; a huge sense of achievement by the group; amazement at having come so far with these techniques; bonding and interaction.

Flag Up: They did well; the courage to take risks; the magic of the moment; the creative genius waiting to get out of us all.

Business Benefits: Using a shared set of guidelines to create and collaborate under pressure - "If we can do that in six minutes, with no script, then what else could we achieve?" The power of storytelling to engage an audience; the strength of a team working together on the edge and the immense value of enjoying what you do.

So we have come to the end of the practical part. I hope you give this a go and make loads of mistakes and laugh a lot. We shall pause for a few reflections before the final part, which will give a list of resources to make your journey more enjoyable and productive.

Beyond Duality

One of the deepest traps that Western thinking has fallen into over the past few centuries is dualistic thinking, which is the habit of slicing and dicing all of life's richness into binary pairs. I touched on this earlier in the chapter *The Task in Hand.*

We are deeply programmed to process information in this way. Here's a few examples just off the top of my head,

Be an artist *vs* make a decent living

Labour *vs* Conservative

Democrat *vs* Republican

Mind *vs* body

Guilty *vs* innocent

Saint *vs* sinner

Mac *vs* PC

Communist *vs* capitalist

Spend *vs* invest

So many of our systems, including education, legal, judicial, political and economic spend vast amounts of time, energy and talent in using duality as a decision making process and a window to view the world.

One of the many benefits of comedy is that we are liberated from duality when we laugh at the absurdity of it. Humour has been defined as "An impression falling on two parts of the brain at the same time" and the laughter produced is a release of the tension that comes from trying to fit one idea in two boxes simultaneously.

Here's a bad joke – Why don't cannibals eat clowns?

Answer – Because they taste funny.

The word funny has landed in two places at once. It claims and seems to explain why, but it does not explain why, because it is the wrong type of funny.

Comedy opens up our thinking, exercises our bodies and helps our hearts to connect to other people. Victor Borge said "Laughter is the shortest distance between two people." Improvising comedy brings us more fully into the present moment and gives us endless opportunities to make our own entertainment, to reclaim our innate gifts, enliven our workplaces, inspire schoolchildren, challenge the dullness of institutions and live richer lives.

The improvisation community is growing worldwide, as more people reach out to each other for a more real and immediate experience. Hollywood is hoping to release some three dimensional movies soon. How about, we give them a miss and spend more time in three dimensional real lives instead?

The last part of this book is a list of resources that have helped many people to have a more vibrant journey through life. Check out the ones that appeal and give them a whirl or don't. It doesn't matter which choice you make, because it's impossible to do this wrong and you're doing brilliantly. Enjoy the ride.

Here's my email address if you want to get in touch: creative@johncremer.co.uk

Act Three

RESOURCES

Books I can highly recommend

Improvisation books

Impro by Keith Johnstone.
A classic work by a pioneer in improvisation.

Everything's An Offer by Robert Poynton.
A delight to read; warm and crystal clear with integrity.

Improvise by Mick Napier.
Superb insights from the founder of the *Annoyance Theatre* in Chicago.

Truth in Comedy by Del Close and Charna Halpern.
Another classic by two masters of improvisation.

The Improv Handbook by Tom Salinsky and Deborah Frances-White.
A goldmine of information for improvisers of all levels of experience.

The Power of Now by Eckhart Tolle.
A lucid exploration of the nature of presence and attention.

Related Topics

There Is Nothing Wrong With You by Cheri Huber.
A wise and compassionate dismantling of the inner critic written from a Buddhist perspective.

The Chalice and the Blade by Raine Eisler.
An eye opening view of our limited understanding of human history with deep insight into the true nature of collaboration.

The Drama of Being a Child by Dr Alice Miller.
A psychoanalyst explores how children lose contact with their vitality and creativity.

Reading People by John Cremer.
Understanding yourself and others using ancient wisdom.
www.readingpeople-johncremer.com

The Artist's Way by Julia Cameron.
A workbook for recovering your creative self, used successfully by many artists and performers.

The Woodland House by Ben Law.
A masterpiece of commitment, determination, improvisation and connecting with like minded people.

Movies

The following films by Mike Leigh:

Life is Sweet
High Hopes
Secrets and Lies
Topsy Turvy
Career Girls

Mike Leigh uses lengthy improvisations to create deeply authentic and compelling films.

Christopher Guest films:

This is Spinal Tap
Waiting for Guffman

There are strong elements of improvisation in both the above films, extremely funny.

Harolde and Maude
Starring Bud Cort and Ruth Gordon. Not improvised, just very funny and life affirming.

Withnail and I
Starring Richard E Grant, Richard Griffiths, Paul McGann. Just painfully funny, a gem.

Every *Monty Python* Film or TV Episode, obviously.

Improvisation teachers I have worked with

Steve Roe. Steve founded *Hoopla Impro* in London and is a relentless bundle of warmth and joy. His enthusiasm and willingness to learn make him a fine teacher. **www.hooplaimpro.com**

Sprout Ideas. Gentle warm teaching style, lovely chaps **www.sproutideas.co.uk**

Annoyance Theatre. Full-on maverick improvisers, not for the faint hearted or newcomers, loads of fun pushing the boundaries.
www.annoyanceproductions.com

Marshal Stern and Nancy Howland-Walker. Fabulous, positive teachers of improvised song and Zenprov – a mindful approach to improvisation.
www.chicagoimprovassociates.com

Bill Arnett. Outstanding and quirky teacher with clear practical feedback. The Maydays had classes with him at Improv Olympic and brought him to England to share his wisdom.
www.improvolymp.com

Kate Hilder. Kate teaches *Action Theatre*, not improvised comedy but a way of connecting with yourself through authentic spontaneous movement.
She still doesn't have a website!

Other Resources

Osho Leela is the UKs leading personal development and active meditation centre; a thriving community in beautiful Dorset countryside. A place to relax and unwind or dive in to some intense workshops.
www.osholeela.co.uk

Applied Improvisation Network. An online community of improvisers worldwide who are dedicated to spreading the benefits of improvisation.
www.appliedimprov.ning.com

Learn Improv. Massive online resource for exercises, tips and tools.
www.learnimprov.com

The Maydays. Brighton based troupe performing long form, short form, improvised songs and all points in between. We teach courses from beginning to performance, bespoke workshops for businesses and organisations. Every Thursday at 7.30pm we still teach a drop-in class, all are welcome.
www.themaydays.co.uk

the MAYDAYS

The award winning improvisation troupe.
Let them create a hilarious bespoke experience for **your** event.

The Maydays can provide anything from a 30 minute intimate "unplugged" performance up to a 90 minute extravaganza including an improvised musical and onstage appearances by audience members. Every show is geared to the needs of the client; taking into account such variables as level of interaction, purpose of the event, age range of audience, appropriate content etc.

They also offer training sessions in improvisation skills which are designed to unlock the creativity of a team and have huge amounts of fun in the process. Anyone can have a go and the laughter generated is highly infectious.

www.themaydays.co.uk

ABOUT THE AUTHOR

John Cremer is a speaker, trainer and improviser. He has taught and performed improvisation over 15 years and has refined his methods by working with a huge range of clients.

Initially grabbed and inspired by the sheer joy of improvising onstage he has since devoted time and energy to the practical and philosophical applications of improvisation principles. John finds these new connections and deeper insights enrich his personal and professional life every day.

His journey in personal development began in Phoenix Arizona in 1985 with Omega Vector, an organisation that offered intensive awareness trainings.

John worked as a trainer in the organisation and went on to work with groups devoted to exploring human potential.

He joined the Oxymorons Improvisation Troupe, directing and performing in hundreds of shows under the guidance of the legendary Louis Anthony Russo and was later invited to join Essential Theatre Playback Company, which gave totally improvised plays based on true tories from audience members.

Returning to the UK in 2001 John founded the Maydays, an award-winning improvisation troupe, and performs with them regularly.

The Maydays give public shows and are renowned for their totally improvised musical numbers. They create bespoke shows and trainings for companies and organisations including Legal and General, the British Council, Friends of the Earth.

They won Best Comedy Show Brighton Festival Fringe 2007.

www.themaydays.co.uk

"The Maydays' performance was the highlight of our 2008 clergy conference - hilarious, clever and pitched perfectly for the audience. They enthralled us by turning our suggestions and comments into comic turns and songs. The laughter never stopped and it was all totally appropriate - slightly cheeky but never offensive. They got the audience on their side from the start, and the mood of happiness and delight lingered long after they'd left the stage."
— The Rt Revd Graham James, Bishop of Norwich

John is a Fellow of the Professional Speakers Association and gives keynote talks and improvisation skills training to companies and organisations such as: T-Mobile, Deloitte, Microsoft, Airbus, Vistage and was awarded Star Speaker 2007 by the Academy for Chief Executives.

When he is not speaking, training, writing, researching or performing he can often be spotted, rod in hand, stalking the elusive sea trout and bass from Brighton beach; he usually catches mackerel.

This material is best-learned first-hand from an experienced practitioner.
John Cremer offers the following to companies and organisations:

IMPROVISATION WORKSHOPS

John Cremer offers training and keynote presentations entitled *The Fine Art of Improvisation.*

This can be offered in the following formats: -

Breakout sessions at a conference from 45-90 minutes. These are highly interactive, fast-paced and utterly hilarious. Delegates also take away potent tools to implement during and after the event.

Half-day training. These sessions are hands-on, enthralling, utterly unique, quite silly and deeply profound in their after effects. These are in high demand for retreats as they create bonding in new groups and transform dynamics in established groups.

Keynote talk with or without bringing audience volunteers onstage for "on the spot" improvisation skills training. These get audiences involved, laughing a lot and thinking along very different lines.

Bespoke improvised comedy shows for any event. This highly interactive presentation gives participants an experience of using techniques which:

- Enhance personal effectiveness and confidence under pressure.

- Access "out of the box" innovative thinking and problem solving.

- Reduce stress levels and misunderstanding by promoting positive interpersonal communication.

- Quickly and deeply bond and inspire a team.

- Create an enjoyable and productive work environment which increases staff retention.

Approach

An experiential process in which simple tools are learned and applied in a series of increasingly challenging exercises. There is laughter galore as participants are taken progressively outside of their comfort zone in a supportive, exciting atmosphere.

The skills acquired are embodied and not just theorised.

The personal and professional benefits and challenges are explored as they arise.

Benefits

The major benefit is, that the group as a whole becomes more bonded, open and supportive – members are very often surprised by the hidden talent of people they have known for years!

Members take away simple, yet highly effective, tools that enable instant access to higher levels of confidence and creative thinking. They learn techniques of brainstorming and problem solving which engage the latent potential of teams.

The group itself often shifts out of habitual dynamics, becoming flexible and more able to address uncomfortable subjects. Often the quiet members speak up more and the noisy ones listen better!

Participants report improved communications with staff and a positive impact on morale and engagement.

Recent clients include: Friends of the Earth, the British Council, Legal and General and Norfolk Diocese Ecclesiastical Conference.

"The techniques of improvisation go straight to the heart of what it takes to be an effective leader. CEO's need to make instant judgements and decisions, often without preparation and then commit to seeing them through. This workshop provides a safe environment where CEO's can practice these skills without fear of failure or ridicule and can even learn to laugh at their mistakes". – Simon Lester: CEO, Lester Hotels Group

Reading People Workshops

1. A half-day Reading People Workshop
for a maximum of twelve participants.

Programme
This system of reading people is revealed in a clear and precise and progressional manner. Each "type" of person is explored in detail, using examples from history, members' own lives and contemporary culture. We look at the typical occupations for each "type" and also, their worst possible jobs. The group creates an ideal company using the system and also finds the precise recipe for business failure - which can be just as useful to know. The relationships and misunderstandings that arise naturally between types are addressed and solutions are explored. Each participant has the option to discover their own type and look at the implications this has in their personal and professional life. Time and willingness permitting, we use role-play and improvisation to experience the nature of one's type.

There is a strong thread of humour running through the session, as nothing is funnier than human nature.

Outcomes
Members come away with practical knowledge of the system and the potential applications. The number of "Ahas" can be extraordinary. The information is fascinating, and for some it is life changing. This system can help put into concrete terms insights we have into others but do not have a context for. On a personal level, members come to greater acceptance of themselves and other people. Once we see the influence one's type has it becomes easy to let go of expecting others to be different.

Professionally the amount of money and energy saved when we find the right type for the job is enormous.

A concise, purpose written workbook that reinforces the learning is available.

2. A full day Reading People Masterclass

This goes deeper into the personal learning and applications of the system. There is time for a question and answer session that facilitates hands-on applications of the system using real life situations.

3. A keynote talk on Reading People

Lively and humorous yet has a profound effect when delegates reflect upon the material. Time permitting, we use volunteers from the audience as examples of types. Visual aids and short movie clips enrich the learning process.

4. Breakout sessions on Reading People for conferences

This adds a completely different dimension to an event, as learning can be put into practice immediately and can be a revelation in large groups.

5. Bespoke Reading People Training

To raise the awareness level of a team, explore habitual dynamics and unlock hidden potential. These are especially powerful when applied for a specific purpose or in a retreat setting. Can be a one-off, a series or ongoing.

"The management team had a great time learning this unique high impact material. They found it eye opening, as well as highly practical in the workplace. We came away with a better understanding of ourselves, our clients and each other. Many in the group found insight into their personal relationships and felt they could now understand their partners and children better."
– Chris Davis, CEO Dunlop Systems & Components Limited

"Content & Presentation: - 10/10. Fantastic, captivating, enthralling, brilliant, would like to do a full day session." – Paul Scanlon, Chairman CDP Print Management

"Thank you for your masterclass performance yesterday. Reading People was a resounding success. Your command of the subject, your inspirational style backed up by your astonishing verbal dexterity made for one of the greatest Academy days I have experienced. One member scored you straight tens, and said it was "the most enjoyable morning that he has had since joining the Academy".
– Joe Adams, Chairman Group 11 Academy for Chief Executives

"This has been without doubt the most worthwhile personnel management and HR/ personal/ professional development course that I have ever attended. John's presentation style is truly inspiring, he engages with participants at a remarkable level. I'm recommending this course to everyone!"
– John Nicholls, MD London Calling Arts

Are you an expert?

Sunmakers can brand your expertise to make it shine

We can make your brand, your website, products, books and ebooks sell for you when you're not there.

We design and publish an eclectic range of books written by leading experts.

Perhaps you should be one of them?

 SUNMAKERS

www.sunmakers.co.uk
+44 (0)1865 779944

NOTES

READING PEOPLE
USING ANCIENT WISDOM
TO UNDERSTAND YOURSELF AND OTHERS

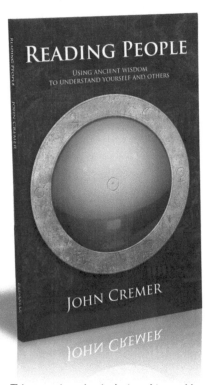

"O would some Power, the gift to give us,
To see ourselves as others see us!
It would from many a blunder free us"
— Robert Burns

One of humanity's strongest desires is to make sense of our place in the cosmos.

Throughout history we have discovered intriguing connections between ourselves, the natural world and the greater whole. We have created models to reflect our understanding of the multi-faceted relationships that we encounter.

Reading People is part of an ancient stream of knowledge that has come to the surface of human awareness at various times in history.

This current version is designed to enable:

- Understanding and compassion for oneself and others.
- Rapid yet penetrating assessment of interpersonal dynamics.
- Deeper appreciation for other cultures and viewpoints.
- Accelerated personal and professional development.
- Opportunities to transform habitual patterns in relationships and families.

For many people this material is fascinating, for some it is life changing. The system is deceptively simple to pick up and use to observe others. Experienced practitioners can read someone at a deep level within seconds of meeting them for the first time. Applying the principles to one's own life requires a lifetime of study and discipline.